High School Leaders And Their Schools

Volume I:
A National Profile

Leonard O. Pellicer

Lorin W. Anderson

James W. Keefe

Edgar A. Kelley

Lloyd E. McCleary

National Association of Secondary School Principals
1904 Association Drive ● Reston, Virginia 22091

Scott D. Thomson, NASSP Executive Director
Thomas F. Koerner, Director of Publications
Patricia Lucas George, Editor
Eugenia Cooper Potter, Technical Editor

Copyright 1988
National Association of Secondary School Principals
1904 Association Drive
Reston, Virginia 22091
(703) 860-0200

IBSN 0-88210-216-8

The Research Team
Leonard O. Pellicer is professor and chair of the Department of Educational
  Leadership and Policies, University of South Carolina.
Lorin W. Anderson is research professor in the Department of Educational
  Leadership and Policies, University of South Carolina.
James W. Keefe is director of research, National Association of Secondary
  School Principals.
Edgar A. Kelley is professor in the Department of Educational Leadership,
  Western Michigan University.
Lloyd E. McCleary is professor of educational administration, University of
  Utah.

The Steering Committee
Patricia Campbell, Lakewood Senior High School, Lakewood, Colorado
Glen M. DeHaven, Oldtown School, Oldtown, Maryland
Richard A. Gorton, University of Wisconsin-Milwaukee
Jacqueline H. Simmons, Paul Robeson High School, Chicago, Illinois
Norman O. Stevens, Mill River Union High School, North Clarendon, Vermont
Michael K. Thomas, Vashon High School, St. Louis, Missouri
Peggy P. Walters, J. Frank Dobie High School, Houston, Texas
Gary P. Wells, Henley High School, Klamath Falls, Oregon
Jeannette M. Wheatley, Cass Technical High School, Detroit, Michigan
James V. Wright, Fremont Ross High School, Fremont, Ohio

Contents

Tables

Additional tables are located in Appendix B, beginning on page 143. These supplementary tables are cited in the text with an "A" (e.g., 1.1A). A complete list of these tables appears at the beginning of Appendix B.

Preface

Principals set the tone of schools. They determine, in large measure, the environment for students. They are also closely involved with communities. We at Carnegie have found that every successful school has a thoughtful, hardworking, and committed principal in charge.

This NASSP survey, now in its third cycle, brings us intimately into the world of principals. For example, today's principals feel the need for more drug and alcohol education programs. They are acutely aware of the social difficulties young people bring with them to school. They understand the need for a culturally diverse citizenship education program. Their commitment to educate *all* students is more intense than ever.

While principals have more paperwork and more externally imposed regulations, they continue to feel positive about their work. They are, in fact, increasingly optimistic about their ability to shape and sustain successful schools. Further, today's principals are comfortable with teachers and understand the importance of cooperative decision making.

Other trends revealed in this report, however, give cause for some concern. I'm troubled, for example, that secondary school principals remain predominantly white and male. There has, in fact, been little shift in the diversity of school leadership over the past 20 years. Positive steps must be taken to ensure that the principalship becomes more representative of the changing demography of the nation.

I am also concerned about the continued erosion of parent involvement in schools. To be sure, a host of social and economic circumstances have contributed to the growing gap between the home and school. However, school leaders have a special obligation to build partnerships with parents and to involve them more fully in the education of their children.

This survey of the life and work of principals contributes significantly to the growing literature on the condition of public education. I applaud the richness of the data and recommend that the findings of this report be used as the basis for an ongoing examination of the principal as the key to school renewal. Indeed, it is my firm conviction that education in America will be strengthened only as we strengthen management at the local school and give principals the authority they need to lead.

Ernest L. Boyer
President
The Carnegie Foundation for the
Advancement of Teaching

Introduction

The introduction to Volume I of NASSP's comprehensive study of the high school principalship in 1978 included the statement, "The principalship today is not the principalship of 1965, nor will it be the principalship of 1985." These words underscore the dynamic nature of the senior high school principalship and form the basis for the NASSP's enduring commitment to regular and systematic monitoring of the principalship through major studies of the kind reported in the following pages.

This study is the third in a series of national studies of the high school principalship dating back to the early 1960s. Each study has represented an attempt to build a knowledge base about the senior high school principalship by systematically gathering, organizing, and presenting a large amount of descriptive data and then investigating several important aspects of the principalship not yet fully explored.

The major purpose of this study was to analyze and describe high school leaders and their schools. The focus of the present study has been broadened beyond that of its antecedents to include both the major roles in building administration: the principalship and the assistant principalship. For the first time, descriptive data have been gathered, analyzed, and reported about principals and assistant principals in the same schools. This expanded treatment represents researchers' awareness of the complexity of the principalship and the importance of the entire administrative team that functions together to organize, administer, and lead American high schools.

The research questions that guided the study were:

1. What are the personal and professional characteristics, job-related tasks, and expectations of senior high school principals and assistant principals?
2. What similarities and differences exist in the characteristics, tasks, and expectations of principals and assistant principals considering grade levels administered and selected demographic characteristics of the schools?
3. What are the characteristics of senior high school staffs, students, and communities?
4. What variations exist in senior high school organizational structures and instructional programs?
5. What similarities and differences exist in senior high school programs considering grade level organization and selected demographic characteristics of the schools?
6. What are the views of senior high school principals and assistant principals on selected educational issues and trends?

1

7. What indices (characteristics and behaviors) of high performing and typically performing principals are related to school effectiveness?

8. What are the administrative and programmatic similarities and differences between effective schools administered by principals described as "high performers" and those administered by "typical" principals?

Answers to the first six questions are the substance of this volume. Questions 7 and 8 are explored in phase two of the study.

Design of the Study

The study was conducted by a research team with the advice and assistance of a steering committee composed of four senior high school assistant principals, three large-school senior high principals, two small-school senior high principals, and a professor of educational leadership. The research team and steering committee met together during the early stages of the study to discuss objectives, clarify research questions, and review the survey instruments.

One of the major problems the research team faced was the length of the survey instruments. With each succeeding national survey, the bulk of the questions from the previous survey were retained while numerous others were added to reflect the issues and interests of the particular decade studied. The present study was no exception. To further compound the problem, a whole series of questions related to the assistant principalship was added to study the major actors of the high school principalship team simultaneously.

To address the problem of length, three forms of the survey instrument were developed for use with principals and two forms for assistant principals. A common core of demographic questions was incorporated in all forms, while the remaining questions were divided equally among the related forms. An attempt was made to group these questions by similarity of topic. All career questions, for example, were included in form A of the principal's survey, and school programmatic questions in form C. Whenever possible, the questions of the 1987 survey were designed to permit comparisons with data from the previous national studies of 1965 and 1977. Despite the attempts to shorten the survey instruments, the resulting forms were still quite lengthy. This may account, in part, for the somewhat lower than hoped-for return on the national sample.

A sample of 1,208 secondary schools was randomly drawn from NASSP's national database of all American schools with grade 12. A survey form for the principal and a survey form for one assistant principal were mailed to each of the 1,208 schools in early 1987. From this initial mailing, 531 principal surveys and 347 assistant principal surveys were returned. A preliminary analysis of returned questionnaires indicated a disproportionate response rate, primarily from smaller schools in the Midwest. The lower percentage of assistant principal returns, in particular, probably reflected this skew toward small schools, many of which do not have assistant principals. Ironically, later investigation revealed that this initial pattern of returns, while idiosyncratic, was very similar to the 1977 response.

A second set of surveys was mailed in late March of 1987. These surveys, although randomly selected, were targeted by zip codes to redress the imbalance in preliminary returns. Larger metropolitan areas in several states received the bulk of the second sampling. Three hundred thirty-six survey instruments were mailed; 185 returns were received from principals and 162 from assistant principals. In all, 1,544 survey instruments were sent; 716 were returned by principals and 509 by assistant principals. The response rate for principals was 46 percent. The response rate for assistant principals cannot be calculated precisely, since many surveys were mailed to schools without an assistant principal. Tables 0.1A through 0.7A, located in Appendix B, give detailed information on the demographic characteristics of the sample. The data generated from this national survey of school leaders provide the basis for this report.

Organization of the Report

Unquestionably, senior high school administrators occupy positions of critical importance in the nation's schools. What these persons do and how they manage to meet their innumerable responsibilities are of vital interest to aspiring school leaders, current practitioners, professors of preservice programs, and officials who establish certification guidelines.

The data presented in this report offer a picture of American high school leaders and their schools in 1987. Whenever possible, the data collected in this study have been compared with the data of previous studies to develop a longitudinal perspective on the constantly changing roles of high school leaders. The principalship of 1987 is not the same as the principalship of 1977 or 1965. Surely, it will not be the same in 1997.

Chapter I presents a discussion of characteristics and opinions of school leaders. Chapter II is devoted to the tasks and problems of school leaders, while Chapter III is concerned with educational programs and issues. Chapter IV offers a picture of the contributions of assistant principals, and Chapter V explores the principalship as a career. The final chapter presents summary profiles of high school leaders and their schools.

Characteristics and Opinions of High School Leaders

An initial step in understanding high school principals and assistant principals is to describe who they are and what they believe about basic educational issues and problems. In this chapter, data about the sex, age, ethnicity, salaries, contracts, and professional and civic activities of high school leaders are presented. Their opinions on such topics as administrative tenure, principal certification, and broad educational issues are documented. Where appropriate, comparisons are drawn between the current data and those presented in the 1965 and 1977 reports.

CHARACTERISTICS OF SCHOOL LEADERS

In general, most principals and assistant principals are white males receiving salaries of at least $30,000. They are not tenured but have single-year contracts; they do receive medical, retirement, life insurance, and dental benefits. Despite these generalizations, however, differences among principals and assistant principals do exist.

Sex of Principals and Assistant Principals

About one out of every eight principals is female, a higher number than that reported in 1977, but only slightly higher than in 1965 (Table 1.1A). A greater percentage of assistant principals, almost one-fifth, are female (Table 1.2), suggesting the potential for more women entering the high school principalship as senior male principals retire during the next few years.

Female principals and assistant principals are more common in certain regions of the country than in others (Tables 1.3A and 1.4A). On the West Coast, 20 percent or more of principals and assistant principals are female. Similarly, more than 20 percent of the assistant principals in New England and in the South are female.

TABLE 1.2
Distribution of Principals and Assistant Principals by Sex*

Sex	Principals	Asst. Principals
Female	12	18
Male	88	82

*All tables represent percentages unless otherwise noted.

4

In contrast, fewer than 10 percent of the principals in New England, the Southwest, and the mountain region are female. The smallest percentages of female assistant principals are also found in the Mountain region and the Southwest.

Female principals and assistant principals are more common in certain size communities than in others (Table 1.5A). In general, the larger the community population, the more likely there will be a female principal or assistant principal. In cities with populations of one million or more, for example, about 1 of every 3 principals and assistant principals is female. In smaller cities, towns, and rural areas, no more than 1 in 10 principals and 1 in 6 assistant principals is female.

Female principals and assistant principals are also more common in certain types of schools than in others (Table 1.6A). In all school types, with the exception of public comprehensive schools, more than one in five principals is female. In public alternative schools, female principals are in the majority. The pattern is similar for assistant principals, except that in public alternative schools, all responding assistant principals are male. In public specialized, private religious, and private non-religious schools, more than one-third of the assistant principals are female.

In public comprehensive schools, however, only 1 in 12 principals and 1 in 6 assistant principals is female. These figures are particularly significant to the survey since more than 4 of 5 principals and assistant principals responding to the survey were employed in public comprehensive schools.

Age of Principals and Assistant Principals

Both principals and assistant principals vary widely across the age spectrum (Tables 1.7A and 1.8). The major change in the ages of principals over the past two decades is a decrease in those who are younger than 35. At the same time, however, the percentage of principals who are 55 years and older first decreased from 1965 to 1977 and then increased from 1977 to the present (a net decrease of 4 percent). Possible explanations for and consequences of these changes are discussed in Chapter 5.

Predictably, assistant principals are somewhat younger than principals, but the age differences are not as great as might be expected. Eighty percent of the principals and 82 percent of the assistant principals are between 35 and 54 years of age. A slightly higher percentage of principals are older than 54, while a slightly higher percentage of assistant principals are younger than 35.

TABLE 1.8
Distribution of Principals and Assistant Principals by Age

	24–29	30–34	35–39	40–44	45–49	50–54	55–59	60+
Principals	0	3	16	24	21	19	11	5
Asst. Principals	1	7	21	26	19	16	8	3

The average ages of principals and assistant principals also vary by the regions of the country (Table 1.9A). More than two in five principals in the Mid-Atlantic and Mountain regions are 50 years old or older. In the South, by contrast, only one in every four is 50 years old or older. The largest percentages of younger principals are found in the South, New England, and the Mountain regions.

The West Coast has the largest percentage of assistant principals over 50 years of age (almost 40 percent), while three of five assistant principals in New England are in their 40s. The percentages of younger assistant principals are comparable across all regions, with the exception of New England.

The average ages of principals and assistant principals also differ according to the size of the community in which their schools are located (Table 1.10A). In general, the smaller the community, the younger the principal and assistant principal. For example, more than one-fourth of the principals in small cities, towns, and rural areas are younger than 40. By contrast, almost two-thirds of the principals in cities with populations of one million or more and more than one-half of the principals in cities with populations between 150,000 and one million are 50 years or older.

For assistant principals, the trend is not quite as clear. The majority of assistant principals in all population categories except small cities, towns, and rural areas are in their 40s. In the small cities, towns, and rural areas, two in every five assistant principals are younger than 40. In larger cities, almost twice as many assistant principals are 50 or older than are younger than 40.

These data suggest that small cities, towns, and rural areas may serve as "proving grounds" for high school administrators. Those hiring administrators for high schools in larger cities want experienced persons. Schools in small cities, towns, and rural areas provide candidates for these large city positions.

Ethnicity of Principals and Assistant Principals

Just as the vast majority of principals and assistant principals are male, they also are white (Tables 1.11A and 1.12). In this regard, two points are noteworthy. First, there has been a substantial increase in Hispanic principals during the past 10 years, although both their actual number and percentage remain small. (A similar increase in Hispanic assistant principals

TABLE 1.12
Ethnic Distribution of Principals and Assistant Principals

	White	Black	Hispanic	American Indian	Asian	Other
Principal	93.7	3.8	1.7	.1	.4	.3
Asst. Principal	88.5	9.5	1.4	.2	.2	.2

6

is not evident.) Second, there has been a substantial increase in the number of black assistant principals during the same time period. Black assistant principals account for almost 10 percent of all assistant principals. (Comparable increases in black principals are not evident.) In total, there are almost three times as many Hispanic principals and black assistant principals as there were 10 years ago.

Regionally, vast differences exist in the percentages of non-white principals and assistant principals. These differences quite likely reflect variations in the ethnic composition of the overall population (Table 1.13A). In New England and the Mountain region, for example, all the principals who responded to the survey are white. In the Southwest and on the West Coast, however, more than 10 percent of the principals are non-white. The highest percentages of non-white assistant principals are in the South (24 percent) and Southwest (18 percent). By contrast, few if any non-white assistant principals are employed in New England, the Midwest, and the Mountain regions.

Large differences in the percentages of non-white principals and assistant principals also exist across different community populations (Table 1.14A). Stated simply, the larger the community, the more likely the community is to have a non-white principal or assistant principal. The largest percentages of non-white principals and assistant principals work in cities with populations greater than 150,000. In these communities, more than one-sixth of the principals and one-fifth of the assistant principals are non-white. In rural areas, towns, and small cities, on the other hand, 12 percent or fewer of the principals and assistant principals are non-white.

Salaries of Principals and Assistant Principals

Salaries of principals have not changed greatly over the past decade when adjusted for inflation (Table 1.15).

While substantial increases in salaries are evident between 1965 and 1977, increases between 1977 and 1987 are quite small. Despite this apparent stabilization of salaries, the principals in this survey (compared with those surveyed in 1977) reported more satisfaction with their jobs,

TABLE 1.15
Longitudinal Comparison of Principals' Salaries
(Adjusted for Inflation)

Salary Range	1987	Salary Range[1]	1977	Salary Range[1]	1965
Less than $29,999	9	Less than $29,195	6	Less than $28,067	46
$30,000–44,999	45	$29,197–43,793	48	$28,070–43,856	43
$45,000 or more	44	$43,796 or more	40	$43,860 or more	10

Notes: (1) Salary ranges for 1977 and 1965 converted to 1987 dollars. Source: *Economic Report of the President*, 1987 edition; U.S. Government Printing Office, Washington, D.C., 1987; Table B55, p. 307.

(2) Responses for category "Does Not Apply—Religious Order" have been dropped. Columns in the table total less than 100 percent because of this omission.

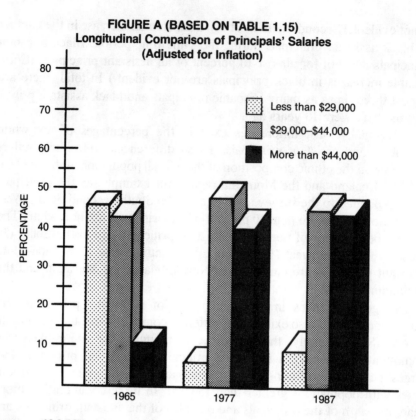

FIGURE A (BASED ON TABLE 1.15)
Longitudinal Comparison of Principals' Salaries
(Adjusted for Inflation)

Legend:
- Less than $29,000
- $29,000–$44,000
- More than $44,000

Y-axis: PERCENTAGE

X-axis: 1965, 1977, 1987

more self-fulfillment, and less restriction from outside forces on their capability to perform their jobs. (See Chapter 2.) Current salaries apparently satisfy incumbents, but may present problems in the recruitment of new administrative personnel.

There were rapid salary increases from 1965 to 1977 but almost no real increases from 1977 to 1987. As a result, the salary differential between teachers and principals has narrowed since 1977. The average principal salary minus the average teacher salary is now less than it was 10 years ago. At the same time, expenditure per pupil has doubled (since 1977).

As might be expected, principals are paid more than assistant principals (Table 1.16). Almost three times as many principals as assistant principals report receiving annual salaries of $45,000 or more.

When asked about their salary determination, almost one-half of the principals and slightly more than one-half of the assistant principals indicated that salaries were determined either by the school board or by a formal bargaining group (Table 1.17A). A larger percentage of principals than assistant principals reported that salary was determined by informal negotiation with the board, either as a member of an administrative group or individually.

Salaries of both principals and assistant principals increase with age (Table 1.18A). Through age 40, principals and assistant principals receive similar salaries. Beyond age 40, however, the salaries of the majority of

8

TABLE 1.16
Salaries of Principals and Assistant Principals

Salary Range	Principals	Asst. Principals
Less than $25,000	4	8
$25,000–29,999	5	9
$30,000–34,999	12	19
$35,000–39,999	14	23
$40,000–44,999	19	22
$45,000–49,999	16	9
$50,000–54,999	15	6
$55,000–59,999	6	3
$60,000 or more	7	

Notes: (1) Asst. Principal lowest range (8%) collapsed from "<$20,000" (3%) and "$20,000–24,999" (5%).
(2) Asst. Principal upper range (3%) actually "$55,000 or more."

assistant principals range from $30,000 to $44,999, while the majority of principals receive salaries of $45,000 or more. In all probability, assistant principals receive smaller annual salary increments than principals in the post-40 age group.

Non-white principals receive higher salaries than white principals (Table 1.19A). Such is not the case, however, for non-white assistant principals. More than three-fourths of the non-white principals, in contrast with slightly less than one-half of the white principals, receive annual salaries of $45,000 or more. This salary differentiation cannot be explained by differences in age, since the average ages of white and non-white principals are quite similar. On the other hand, it may be attributed to region (with the highest percentage of non-white principals on the West Coast) or school size (with the highest percentage of non-white principals from large schools in large cities).

Principals' and assistant principals' salaries vary across the geographic regions of this country (Table 1.20A and 1.21A). The highest salaries for principals and assistant principals are found in the Mid-Atlantic and West Coast regions. In these two regions, fewer than 10 percent of the principals receive salaries less than $35,000. Forty-nine percent of the principals in the Mid-Atlantic region and 52 percent on the West Coast receive salaries in excess of $50,000. Similarly, fewer than 10 percent of the assistant principals in these two regions receive salaries less than $30,000; approximately one in six receive salaries of $50,000 or more.

Principal salaries in the remaining regions are comparable, with slightly higher salaries in the Midwest and Southwest. For assistant principals, however, two additional regional discrepancies are worth noting. First, about 1 in 10 assistant principals in the Southwest receives a salary of $50,000 or more, a finding that appears unrelated to age. Second, one-third of the assistant principals in the South receive annual salaries less than $30,000. Only 2 percent of the assistant principals in this region receive salaries of more than $45,000. This finding may reflect the somewhat younger age of assistant principals in this region.

9

Comparisons of salaries received by male and female principals produce somewhat confusing results (Table 1.22A). A disproportionate number of females receive salaries less than $30,000; they are more likely to be principals of parochial or private high schools. By contrast, a disproportionate number of females receive salaries between $50,000 and $60,000; they are more likely to be principals of public alternative or public specialized schools. Similarly, disproportionate percentages of female assistant principals receive the lowest salaries (less than $25,000) or salaries ranging from $55,000 to $59,999. In interpreting these data, however, keep in mind that the actual number of female assistant principals in the upper categories is quite small.

Finally, principals' and assistant principals' salaries differ according to the size of their schools (Table 1.23A). Stated simply, the larger the school, the higher the salary. Almost three-fourths of the principals receiving salaries less than $30,000 administered schools with student enrollments less than 500. Conversely, more than 90 percent of the principals receiving salaries of $50,000 or more were employed in schools with enrollments of at least 1,000 students.

Fringe Benefits, Contracts, and
Activities of Principals and Assistant Principals

The majority of principals and assistant principals receive medical, retirement, life insurance, dental, and auto expense benefits. About 90 percent of the principals have medical benefits and slightly more than two-thirds have retirement benefits (Table 1.24A). On the other hand, fewer than 1 in 5 principals and assistant principals receives tuition for college coursework. Fewer than 1 in 10 principals receives an expense account (or meals), while fewer than 1 in 20 receives housing or tuition for dependents. About 1 in 20 principals and assistant principals receives no benefits at all. In general, the fringe benefits received by the principals and assistant principals are quite similar, but fewer assistant principals are accorded automobile or mileage benefits and expense accounts.

Principals are more likely to receive longer contracts than are assistant principals (Table 1.25A). Almost three-fifths of principals hold 12-month contracts, while only about one-third of assistant principals have them. Few principals or assistant principals have contracts for fewer than 10 months. Almost three-fifths of the principals and two-thirds of the assistant principals hold single-year contracts (Table 1.26A). Only about 1 in 20 principals and assistant principals has a contract for more than three years.

Most (75 percent) principals and assistant principals *do not hold* tenure as administrators. Interestingly, two-thirds of the principals believe that they *should* have administrative tenure.

About one-third of all principals and assistant principals do not belong to any civic organizations (Table 1.27A). Fewer than one in five is a member of three or more civic organizations. Eighty-five percent of the principals and 65 percent of the assistant principals are members of NASSP (Table 1.28A).

More than 7 in 10 principals and assistant principals receive time off to engage in professional development activities (Table 1.29A). Slightly more than one-half of the principals and assistant principals reported that the district pays all or most of the expenses for these activities. Fewer than one-half of the principals and one-third of the assistant principals reported that the district pays their membership dues for professional associations and organizations. About 1 in 20 principals and assistant principals said that he or she is actually discouraged from participating in professional development activities.

OPINIONS OF SCHOOL LEADERS

Eighty percent or more of the principals selected the following five requirements as ideal for principal certification:

- Specific administrative courses
- A teaching certificate
- A specific number of years of teaching experience
- Specific curriculum development and instruction courses, and
- A master's degree (Table 1.30).

These requirements are also endorsed by more than 70 percent of the assistant principals.

In contrast, fewer than 40 percent of the principals and one-fourth of the assistant principals believe that principal certification should depend on participation in an assessment center, the monitoring of performance after placement, a written professional examination, or a post-master's degree. Both principals and assistant principals moderately support internship

TABLE 1.30
Opinions of Principals and Assistant Principals About Requirements for Principal Certification

Requirement	Principal	Assistant Principal
Specific Administrative Courses	91	87
Teaching Certificate	90	82
Specific Number of Years of Teaching Experience	86	82
Specific Curriculum Dev. & Instruction Courses	84	74
Master's Degree	80	81
Internship	66	59
Specific Non-Administrative Education Courses	50	40
Assessment Center	37	22
Monitoring After Placement	34	24
Professional Examination	22	12
Post-Master's Degree	16	7

experiences, but offer less support of specific non-administrative education courses. In general, both principals and assistant principals endorse the more "traditional" certification requirement while expressing less support for more contemporary elements such as assessment center performance and on-the-job monitoring. Principals' and assistant principals' beliefs about broad educational issues have changed dramatically during the past two decades. Indeed, 6 of the 10 issues ranked most highly by principals and assistant principals in this survey were not even included in the past two surveys (Table 1.31).

These issues include instruction on alcohol and drug abuse, teacher evaluation, computer competence, diagnostic-prescriptive instructional strategies, more stringent requirements in traditional academic subjects, and teacher incentives. More than 50 percent of the principals and assistant principals confirmed the importance of these issues.

Support for three of the broad educational issues has increased during the past two decades:

- The importance of the principle of universal education
- Limitations on classroom discussion of political "isms" and "anti-isms"
- The need to justify each high school subject as practical.

The universal education principle topped the poll for the first time.

On several issues, the current opinions of principals are more like those of their 1965 counterparts than those in 1977. These issues include the reduction or elimination of specific job training in the schools (endorsed by only 10 percent of the principals in the 1977 survey but by more than one-half in the 1965 and 1987 surveys), the requirement that disinterested or hostile youth must attend school (more than one-half of the principals in the 1965 and 1987 surveys but only about 40 percent in 1977), and the requirement that school attendance be mandatory until age 18 or high school graduation (more than one-third in the 1965 and 1987 surveys but only 15 percent in 1977).

On other issues, however, current opinions are more like 1977 than 1965. For example, only one in five principals in 1965 endorsed the need for programs for academically talented students, but more than 90 percent supported them in 1977 and 1987. Four in five principals in 1965 endorsed ability grouping, but only about one-half believed such grouping to be desirable in 1977 and 1987. Similarly, while only one in six principals in 1965 believed that "schools require far too little academic work of students," more than one-half in 1977 and almost one-half in 1987 believed the statement to be true.

Finally, fewer than one-third of all principals during the past two decades agree that "school attendance should be compulsory until high school graduation or age 18," that "the academic year (compulsory) should

TABLE 1.31

Beliefs of Principals and Assistant Principals About Broad Educational Issues

	1987 Prin.	1987 Asst.P.	1977 Prin.	1965 Prin.
The principle of *universal* education is essential to American society.	94	91	81	76
School programs should include specific instruction on alcohol and drug abuse.	92	94	NA	NA
High schools should develop special programs for educating academically talented students.	92	91	92	19
Specific criteria, based on teaching effectiveness research, should be regularly employed in teacher evaluation.	89	91	NA	NA
Functional computer competence is essential for all students.	69	74	NA	NA
High schools should design special programs for the handicapped, ethnic minority, and non-English-speaking.	65	69	75	NA
Schools should implement proven diagnostic-prescriptive strategies to personalize learning for all students.	64	62	NA	NA
More stringent requirements are needed for all students in the traditional academic subjects.	63	68	NA	NA
Various teacher incentives such as differential pay and career ladders should be implemented in place of salary schedules and fixed assignments.	59	53	NA	NA
Grouping according to IQ or achievement scores is desirable in academic subjects such as math, English, and foreign languages.	57	60	53	82
Schools should provide a general intellectual background and leave specific job training to other agencies.	56	45	10	67
Youth who are disinterested or hostile toward schooling should *not* be required to attend.	47	41	59	34
Schools require far too little academic work of students.	46	39	56	16
Certain limitations should be placed upon classroom discussion of political "isms" and "anti-isms."	45	35	39	24
There is a need to justify as practical each subject taught in high schools.	41	43	39	24
Standardized testing of students in all subjects is necessary to improve instruction.	40	45	NA	NA
School attendance should be compulsory until high school graduation, or until age 18.	34	31	15	39
The academic year (compulsory) should be lengthened.	32	26	12	22
Federal aid must be made available to private and religious schools.	22	27	29	19

Notes: Percentages combine "Agree Without Reservation" and "Agree With Some Reservations"; "Do Not Agree" and "Agree With Many Reservations" are omitted from chart.

be lengthened," or that "federal aid must be made available to private and religious schools."

13

Summary

The typical high school principal is a white male between 40 and 55 years of age. The typical high school assistant principal is a white male between 35 and 50 years of age. Females now comprise 18 percent of all assistant principals nationally but only 12 percent of the principals.

After a fairly rapid increase from 1965 to 1977, school administrator salaries have leveled off during the past 10 years. The differential between principal and teacher salaries has narrowed. Few principals or assistant principals hold administrative tenure, but the majority believe that they should.

The vast majority of principals and assistants believe that specific administrative courses, a teaching certificate, teaching experience, a master's degree, specific curriculum and instruction courses, and an internship should be required for principal certification.

The opinions expressed by current principals make it clear that the principalship is changing. Many of the educational issues reported by a large percentage of current principals were not even included in previous surveys. Unfortunately, the broad pattern of this change is not clear. Its complexity will be further examined in subsequent chapters.

II Tasks and Problems of School Leaders

To do their jobs and do them well, principals and assistant principals must accomplish a variety of tasks and solve a number of problems. In this chapter we examine the roles and responsibilities assumed by these school leaders, the problems and issues they confront, and the satisfaction they receive from their jobs. The data in this chapter were reported primarily by principals; data collected from assistant principals are included whenever they are available.

ROLES AND RESPONSIBILITIES

The Ideal Principal

Principals were asked to read three pairs of statements and select from each pair the statement that best characterized the role of the principal. Based on the majority view, the principal "should take initiative in developing and implementing school policy" rather than primarily representing "the interests of parents, leaders, and patrons of the school" and should be more involved in leading the school "in new educational directions" than in managing the "day-to-day affairs of the school." At the same time, however, the principal should involve the faculty in decision making rather than unilaterally establishing the agenda and deciding on the important issues in the school (Table 2.1)..

TABLE 2.1
Roles of the Principal

"The principal should . . ."	Agree
". . . primarily represent the interests of parents, leaders, and patrons of the school."	25
". . . take initiative in developing and implementing school policy according to his or her professional judgment."	75
". . . effectively and efficiently manage the day-to-day affairs of the school."	35
". . . lead the school in new educational directions according to his or her best professional judgment."	65
". . . play the major role in establishing the agenda and deciding the important issues in the school."	18
". . . share decision making with the faculty on important issues."	82

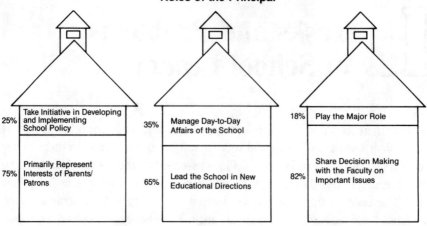

FIGURE B (BASED ON TABLE 2.1)
Roles of the Principal

25% Take Initiative in Developing and Implementing School Policy	35% Manage Day-to-Day Affairs of the School	18% Play the Major Role
75% Primarily Represent Interests of Parents/Patrons	65% Lead the School in New Educational Directions	82% Share Decision Making with the Faculty on Important Issues

Since someone must also attend to the "interests of parents, leaders, and patrons of the school" and the details of the "day-to-day affairs of the school," these responses from principals also point up the need for an administrative team at the building level. As we shall see later in this chapter and in Chapter 4, the assistant principal often assumes these other responsibilities.

Administrative Support

Quite predictably, larger high schools employ more assistant principals (Table 2.2A). In fact, two-thirds of the schools without an assistant principal have student enrollments of fewer than 500. In contrast, more than 9 in every 10 schools that have three or more assistant principals have enrollments of 1,000 or more.

Interestingly, principals in the smallest and largest schools are least satisfied with the administrative support they receive (Table 2.3A). Approximately one-third of the principals in schools with enrollments of fewer than 499 and almost two-fifths of the principals in schools with enrollments of 2,000 or more rate their administrative support as "inadequate." Between one-third and one-half of the principals of the other size schools rate their administrative support as "more than adequate."

Average Work Week

More than one-half of the principals spend a minimum of 55 hours per week on job-related activities (Table 2.4A). During the past two decades, the percentage of principals who work fewer than 50 hours per week has decreased from 25 (in 1965) to 17 (in 1977) to 14 (in 1987). At the same time, the percentage who work more than 60 hours is up slightly from 1977 but down slightly from 1965. In general, the job of the high school principal requires from 50 to 60 hours per week.

16

TABLE 2.5
Average Work Week of Principals and Assistant Principals

Hours Per Week	Principal	Asst. Principal
60 or more	27	12
55 to 59	27	16
50 to 54	32	30
45 to 49	12	25
40 to 44	2	13
Fewer than 40	0	4

As might be expected, principals work more hours per week on the average than do assistant principals (Table 2.5). More than one-half of the principals, in contrast to fewer than one-third of the assistant principals, work 55 hours or more per week. At the other extreme, 17 percent of the assistant principals, but only 2 percent of the principals, work fewer than 45 hours per week.

Principals spend relatively more of their time on school management, personnel, and student activities, and relatively less time on community relations, planning, and professional development (Table 2.6).

Principals believe they should spend relatively more of their time on program development, personnel, and school management, and relatively less time on professional development, student behavior, and working with the district office.

In general, the ways principals spend their time and believe they should spend their time have changed very little during the past decade. The discrepancies between how they spend their time and how they should spend their time that were reported in 1977 still exist. For example, they spend relatively less time on program development and planning and relatively more time on student behavior and working with the district office than they think they should. Apparently, the demands of the job have greater impact on how principals spend their time than do their goals and expectations.

TABLE 2.6
Principals' Time Allocation for a Typical Work Week

	Rank Order			
	Do Spend Time		Should Spend Time	
Area of Responsibility	1987	1977	1987	1977
School Management	1	1	3	3
Personnel	2	2	2	2
Student Activities	3	3	4	4
Program Development	4	5	1	1
Student Behavior	5	4	8	7
District Office	6	6	9	9
Community	7	8	6	8
Planning	8	7	5	5
Professional Development	9	9	7	6

Teaching and Supervisory Responsibilities

Fewer than one in eight principals has some teaching responsibility, a figure that is slightly less than in 1977 and substantially less than in 1965 (Table 2.7A). In 1965, more than one-third of the principals taught at least one course.

Although few principals teach, all principals spend at least some time each week in classrooms (Table 2.8A). More than 20 percent of the principals spend at least seven hours per week informally visiting classrooms. Almost one-half spend between four and six hours per week in this activity. The shift seems to be away from teaching and toward the supervision of teaching.

Principal's Authority

Principal's authority varies greatly in the areas of budget allocation, staffing practices, and staff selection (Table 2.9A). During the past decade, there has been a general decrease in the principal's authority in these areas, particularly in staff selection. But as we shall see, despite these decreases in authority, principals today are somewhat more satisfied with their jobs than they were only a decade ago.

Ten years ago, 9 in every 10 principals had "unrestricted" or "moderately restricted" authority in matters of staff selection. Today, only about two-thirds of all principals have this much authority in staff selection. Decreases in authority in budget allocation and staffing practices are smaller, although notable. The principal's authority is greatest in the allocation of discretionary funds. Principals today have somewhat more authority in this area than they did 10 years ago.

PROBLEMS AND ISSUES

Administrative Roadblocks

"Roadblocks" are conditions that interfere with the ability of principals and assistant principals to do their jobs. More than 70 percent of the principals identified four major roadblocks:

- The amount of time spent on administrative detail
- A general lack of time to do their jobs
- An inability to obtain necessary funds for the operation and improvement of the school
- Apathetic or irresponsible parents (Table 2.10).

Several changes have taken place in the impact of various roadblocks during the past two decades. "Variations in the ability of teachers," "insufficient space and physical facilities," and "problem students" are cited less frequently than they were in the past two surveys.

TABLE 2.10
Administrative Roadblocks for Principals

Problem	1987	1977	1965
Time taken up by administrative detail	83	90	87
Lack of time	79	86	86
Inability to obtain funds	76	79	NA
Apathetic or irresponsible parents	70	79	NA
New state guidelines and requirements	69	NA	NA
Time to administer/supervise student activities	68	NA	NA
Variations in the ability of teachers	64	84	88
Inability to provide teacher time for prof. dev.	62	59	83
Insufficient space and physical facilities	61	66	78
Resistance to change by staff	57	56	64
Problem students	55	76	NA
Defective communications among admin. levels	55	54	41
Longstanding traditions	51	40	47
Collective bargaining agreement	45	41	NA
Teacher tenure	42	50	45
Community pressure	34	NA	NA
Lack of district-wide flexibility	33	35	33
Supt./central office staff do not measure up to expectations	32	38	42
Lack of competent administrative assistance	29	NA	NA
Teacher shortage	29	NA	NA
Lack of competent office help	27	24	46
Lack of opportunity to select staff	21	NA	NA
Teacher turnover	21	NA	NA
Student body too small	20	NA	NA
Lack of content knowledge among staff	16	NA	NA
Student body too large	15	20	NA

Of the nine potential problems/conditions added to the 1987 survey, only two were viewed as actual obstacles by more than one-half of the principals: new state guidelines and requirements (69 percent) and time to administer and supervise student activities (68 percent). The remaining seven ("community pressure," "lack of competent administrative assistance," "teacher shortage," "lack of opportunity to select staff," "teacher turnover," "student body too small," and "lack of content knowledge among staff") were cited as obstacles by 34 percent or less of the principals.

In general, the problems or conditions that assistant principals perceive as roadblocks are similar to those that principals reported (Table 2.11A). Differences of 10 or more percentage points between the responses of principals and assistant principals occurred on only 6 of 26 potential roadblocks. More principals than assistant principals saw "new state guidelines and requirements," "longstanding traditions," and a "student body too small" as obstacles.

More assistant principals saw "staff resistance to change," "problem students," and "lack of opportunity to select staff" as obstacles. That assistant principals see staff and students as more problematic may reflect the types of tasks typically assigned to assistant principals on a daily basis.

19

Collective Bargaining and Interpersonal Relationships

Principals and assistant principals were asked about the status of collective bargaining in their schools and district (Table 2.12A) and the impact of collective bargaining on their relationships with central office administrators and teachers (Table 2.13A). In general, collective bargaining falls into three major categories:

- Not practiced (reported by about 38 percent of the principals)
- For teachers only (reported by about 31 percent)
- For all employees (reported by about 24 percent).

Assistant principals generally agree with these estimates.

It is noteworthy that collective bargaining has not changed principals' relationships with either central office staff members or teachers. Slightly more than three-fourths of the principals who operate under collective bargaining report that it has had no impact on their relationships with central office administrators; almost 7 in every 10 said that it had not affected their relationships with teachers. More principals than assistant principals (12 percent versus 5 percent) feel that collective bargaining detracts from their relationships with teachers. A slightly higher percentage of assistant principals than principals believe that collective bargaining enhances their relationships with both central office administrators and teachers.

Conditions Influencing Schools

Twenty-seven conditions that could conceivably influence schools in the next three to five years were presented to principals. Three-fourths or more of the principals believe that 19 of these conditions will have either a "strong influence" or "some influence" (Table 2.14). Eight-five percent or more believe that the personalized/effective education movement, child abuse (physical, sexual), community participation, community-based learning, and teen sexual activity will exert a significant influence. More than one-third believe that youth gang activity, shifts in enrollment (either up or down), and youth employment will be strong influences. Attention to academic achievement, finance and the general economy, and changing family structure received the least support.

Community Involvement and Interest Groups

Principals are quite clear about those areas in which they believe parents and community should be involved (Table 2.15A). Principals tend to welcome parent and community participation in fund raising, volunteer services, and student discipline and activities. Far fewer principals endorse parent and community involvement in matters of curriculum and instruction, including program development and evaluation, instructional assistance, and student grading. Virtually no principals support parent and community involvement in the selection and evaluation of personnel.

TABLE 2.14
Conditions Influencing Principals

	Total	Strong Influence	Some Influence
Personalized/effective education movement	88	26	62
Child abuse (physical, sexual)	88	18	70
Community participation	86	20	66
Community-based learning	85	32	53
Teen sexual activity	85	17	68
Alcohol abuse	83	20	63
Youth unemployment	82	37	45
Teacher incentives	82	20	62
Teen emotion/psychological problems	81	16	65
Student attendance problems	80	29	51
New technologies	80	19	61
Drug abuse	80	17	63
Graduation requirements	78	25	53
Teacher competency	78	23	55
Demand for basics	78	22	56
Teacher shortage	77	28	49
Teacher motivation	77	21	56
Accountability movement	76	20	56
Student motivation	75	21	54
Youth gang activity	74	49	25
Enrollment decline	73	35	38
Competency testing of students	73	24	49
Enrollment increase	72	39	33
Change in government funding	71	24	47
Changing family structure	68	20	48
Finance and general economy	62	20	42
Attention to academic achievement	56	28	28

Note: Principals were asked to rate which conditions would have influence on *their own school* during the *next three to five years.*

As might be expected, athletic boosters (especially alumni), band and music boosters, and teachers' organizations are the three special interest groups that have the greatest influence on principals (Table 2.16A). Contrary to what is often reported in the media, censorship groups, legal aid groups, extremist individuals or groups, and local labor organizations seem to exert little influence on principals. In fact, the influence of censorship groups and extremist individuals or groups has declined dramatically during the past 25 years.

There have been some interesting changes in the perceived influence of several special interest groups since 1965. Changing influence is particularly evident for state colleges or universities, citizen or parent groups (non-PTA), religious or church groups, and individuals and groups concerned about national reports and school reform. All four of these interest groups exert greater influence today than they did 10 years ago, but about the same degree of influence as they did two decades ago.

In interpreting these changes, it is important to keep in mind that the data reported in 1965 were in fact collected some two years earlier. Perhaps the 1977 survey results reflect the liberal attitudes of the late '60s more accurately than do those of the 1965 survey. If so, the current survey may indicate a return to influence of more traditional social institutions (e.g., universities, churches).

JOB CHARACTERISTICS AND SATISFACTION

Principals today perceive their jobs as having greater job security, with more opportunity to help others, greater prestige, more scope for independent thought and action, and greater self-fulfillment than in the past (Table 2.17). Ratings on these five job characteristics are from 6 to 13 percentage points higher than in 1977, and from 15 to 19 percentage points higher than in 1965. The increases of the past decade are particularly significant, given that principals' salaries stabilized during this time period.

Assistant principals view their jobs much as principals do, with the exception of level of prestige and, to a lesser extent, self-fulfillment (Table 2.18A). Far fewer assistant principals than principals see their jobs as having considerable prestige. And a somewhat larger percentage of the assistant principals (15 percent as compared to 6 percent for principals) feel that their jobs have little self-fulfillment.

The vast majority of principals and assistant principals are "very satisfied" to "satisfied" with their rapport with students, parents, the community, and teachers; with the realization of their expectations; with the

TABLE 2.17
Principals' Ratings of Job Characteristics

Job Characteristic		1987	1977	1965
Job Security:	Little	11	17	26
	Moderate	26	25	24
	Considerable	64	58	49
Opportunity To Help Others:	Little	2	3	8
	Moderate	9	21	21
	Considerable	89	76	71
Prestige:	Little	5	5	14
	Moderate	27	30	37
	Considerable	69	65	50
Independent Thought & Action:	Little	7	12	19
	Moderate	27	34	33
	Considerable	66	54	48
Self-Fulfillment:	Little	6	9	18
	Moderate	28	30	33
	Considerable	66	60	48

Notes: (1) Percentages reflect "actual" ratings of the characteristics; percentages for "ideal" ratings were always higher than the "actual" ratings, but no significant shift occurred in the ideal ratings since 1977.

(2) A five-point scale was used: "Little" combines choices 1 & 2; "Considerable" combines choices 4 & 5.

FIGURE C (BASED ON TABLE 2.17)
Principals' Ratings of Job Characteristics

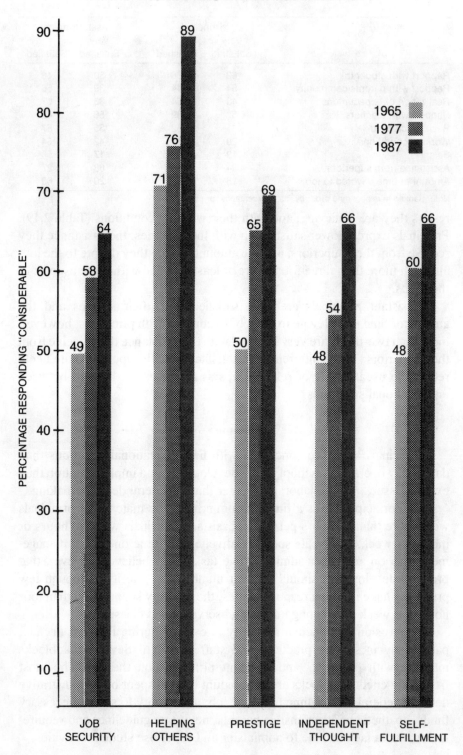

23

TABLE 2.19
Job Satisfaction of Principals and Assistant Principals

	Principal		Asst. Principal	
	Very Satisfied	Satisfied	Very Satisfied	Satisfied
Rapport with students	63	36	50	48
Rapport with parents/community	54	44	39	56
Realization of expectations	43	54	36	57
Rapport with teachers	57	39	56	42
Results achieved	41	52	35	57
Working conditions	29	61	42	54
Salary	19	65	17	56
Assistance from superiors	34	48	68	27
Amount of time devoted to job	15	63	20	63

Note: Ranked in descending order by *total* percentages for principals.

results they are achieving; and with their working conditions (Table 2.19). Principals express lower satisfaction with their salaries, the assistance they receive from their superiors, and the amount of time they devote to the job, although more than three-fourths are at least satisfied with these aspects of their jobs.

Assistant principals are least satisfied with their salaries and the amount of time they devote to the job. In contrast with principals, however, more than two-thirds are very satisfied with the assistance they receive from their superiors. These differences in satisfaction with superiors quite likely reflect the usual nature of relationships as they exist within and between organizational structures.

Summary

Principals are more concerned with new educational directions than day-to-day operations, school policy development and implementation than external issues, and collaborative rather than unilateral decision making.

The principalship is a time-consuming job: the majority of principals work more than 55 hours per week; assistant principals work 50 hours or more per week. Principals spend relatively more time on school management than on any other administrative task. They believe, however, that program development should be their number-one priority. Although few principals have teaching responsibilities, the majority spend more than four hours per week conducting informal observations in classrooms.

An erosion of principal authority is evident during the past decade, particularly in staffing practices and staff selection. Several roadblocks interfere with principals and assistant principals on the job. The most frequently cited roadblocks are the amount of time spent on administrative detail, a general lack of time to do the job, an inability to secure necessary funds, apathetic or irresponsible parents, new state guidelines and requirements, and a lack of time to administer and supervise student activities.

A large number of external factors are likely to affect principals and their schools during the next three to five years. The personalized/effective education movement, child abuse, community participation, community-based learning, and teen sexual activity are chief among them. Athletic, band, and music boosters and teachers' organizations are the special interest groups that exert the greatest influence on principals. The majority of principals believe that parent and community participation should be limited to the more traditional fund raising and volunteer efforts. Few principals support parent/community involvement in matters of curriculum and instruction.

Principals and assistant principals rate their jobs highly in terms of opportunity to help others, job security, prestige, independent thought and action, and self-fulfillment. The ratings on these job characteristics have improved during the past 20 years. Both principals and assistant principals are least satisfied with their salaries and the time they must spend on the job.

III Educational Programs and Issues

Educational programs are the central concern of the high school principal. A number of conditions and issues influence the nature of the programs offered, their management, and their potential to provide a worthwhile secondary education. Data were collected about key conditions and issues, and compared, whenever possible, with data from previous studies. Information is reported in this chapter about student-related factors, teaching staff, educational purposes, the curriculum, program features, and the impact of educational reform.

STUDENT-RELATED FACTORS

Data about student-related factors include per-student expenditure, average daily attendance, student retention (dropout) rate, and percentage of high school graduates entering college. Comparative data are given for each of these variables.

Expenditure per Student

The level of expenditure per student has been shown to correlate positively with independent measures of the quality of educational programs. Per-student expenditure data were collected in comparable studies conducted in 1965 and 1977. These are shown with 1987 data in Table 3.1.

Categories for each of the three studies are not truly comparable because of the changing value of the dollar and real increases in expenditure per student, but some comparisons can be made. About the same percentage of schools fell at the upper end of the distribution in each study. In 1987,

TABLE 3.1
Expenditures per Student

1987		1977		1965	
Less than $1,500	7	Less than $500	3	Less than $30	3
1,500 to 1,999	13	500 to 899	20	30 to 99	6
2,000 to 2,499	22	900 to 1,199	25	100 to 199	8
2,500 to 2,999	22	1,200 to 1,499	28	200 to 299	15
3,000 to 3,499	15	1,500 to 1,799	11	300 to 399	20
3,500 to 3,999	9	1,800 to 2,099	6	400 to 499	15
4,000 to 4,499	5	2,100 to 2,399	4	500 to 599	11
4,500 to 4,999	2	2,400 or more	3	600 to 699	6
5,000 or more	7			700 or more	7

26

fewer than 7 percent of the schools had an expenditure level greater than $5,000 per student; in 1977, 7 percent were more than $2,100; and in 1965, 7 percent exceeded $700. Using 1965 as a base, high-expenditure schools increased these expenses by a factor of 3 in 1977 and by a factor of 7 in 1987. At the lower end of the expenditure scale, 78 percent of the schools in the sample spent less than $1,500 per student in 1977, but only about 7 percent fell in that category by 1987.

Expenditure per student by region is given in Table 3.2A. In the 1987 sample, slightly fewer than 7 percent of the schools spent less than $1,500 per student or more than $5,000. New England and the noncontiguous regions reported no schools in the less than $1,500 category, while the South placed 43 percent of its schools in that category. The Mid-Atlantic and Midwest regions have the highest percentage of schools reporting in the more than $5,000 category. The Midwest and the Mid-Atlantic regions are most strongly represented in the total sample (39 and 16 percent, respectively), but these regions also have the largest number of high schools and do not appear to be over-represented.

Average Daily Attendance (ADA)

The number of students attending school compared to the number actually enrolled is a commonly used statistic, both in school funding formulas and as an index of school health. Considerable improvement in the national average daily attendance (ADA) is apparent from 1977 to 1987 (Table 3.3). In 1987, about 33 percent of the high schools reported more than 95 percent of their students in average daily attendance, versus only 17 percent reporting that level in 1977. Eighty-seven percent of the high schools reported a more than 90 percent attendance rate in 1987, versus 72 percent in 1977. Public health authorities consider a 5 percent absence rate normal for reasons of health.

Retention Rate

The ratio of students who graduate to those who drop out is an index of the holding power of a high school. These data were collected in the 1965 and 1977 studies as well as in 1987. Comparable categories were not used in

TABLE 3.3
Average Daily Attendance

ADA	Schools	
	1987	1977
Fewer than 70		1
70 to 79.9	<1 2	5
80 to 89.9	10	21
90 to 94.9	54	55
More than 95	33	17

TABLE 3.4
Retention Rates of Schools

Retained	1987	1977	1965
More than 95	55		
*90 or more	78	62	54
80 or more	90		
70 or more	95		

*Category of comparable data.

the earlier studies, however, and only the category ''more than 90 percent retained'' is available for comparison.

In 1987, 54 percent of the high schools reported a retention rate greater than 95 percent. In the ''more than 90 percent'' category, a comparison of retention rates for 1987, 1977, and 1965 indicates a steady gain. Put another way, in 1965 only 54 percent of the high schools reported a dropout rate under·10 percent. In 1977 the comparable category was 62 percent, while in 1987 it was 78 percent. It should be pointed out, however, that in 1987 about 10 percent of the high schools still reported a retention rate below 80 percent.

Graduates Entering College

Principals were asked for the percentage of students who go on to college. A significant shift toward greater college matriculation has occurred during the past two decades. The most significant shift occurs in the percentages of high schools with more than 40 percent of their graduates entering college. Table 3.5A shows a change from 37 percent of high schools reporting more than 40 percent in 1965, to 62 percent in 1977, and 75 percent in 1987.

TEACHING STAFF

Principals were asked to rank the importance of certain skills and characteristics in teachers and to report male to female ratios, number of teacher preparations, availability to teachers of subject supervisors, and teacher homeroom responsibilities.

Teacher Skills and Characteristics

Principals were asked to rate 14 commonly accepted skills and characteristics (Table 3.6). The first five rankings in order are:
- Competence in subject matter
- Competence in adjusting instruction to the varying needs of students
- Interpersonal skills in working with students
- Competence in methods of instruction
- Skill in developing positive student self-concept.

TABLE 3.6
Teacher Skills and Characteristics

Skills and Characteristics	Rank
Competence in subject matter knowledge	1
Competence in adjusting instruction to the varying learning styles and learning skills of the students	2
Interpersonal skills in working with students	3
Competence in methods of instruction	4
Skill in developing positive student self-concept	5
Competence in helping student acquire basic learning outcomes	6
Good employee behaviors and work habits (dependability, punctuality, attendance, completion of tasks on time).	7
Ability to model appropriate adult behaviors	8
Interpersonal skills in working with colleagues	9
Sensitivity to differing socioeconomic backgrounds of students	9
Competence in developing and evaluating new instructional techniques	11
Sensitivity to differing cultural backgrounds of students	11
Skill in developing in students respect for others	11
Interpersonal skills in working with parents and citizens	14

Principals showed uniformly high agreement on these five items. Sixty-six percent, for example, judged competence in subject matter as their first, second, or third choice. Fifty-eight percent judged adjusting instruction to student needs as one of their first three choices.

Teacher Preparations

Principals reported the percentage of their teachers who had one, two, three, or four or more course preparations per day (Table 3.7A). Seven

FIGURE D (BASED ON TABLE 3.6)
Teacher Skills and Characteristics

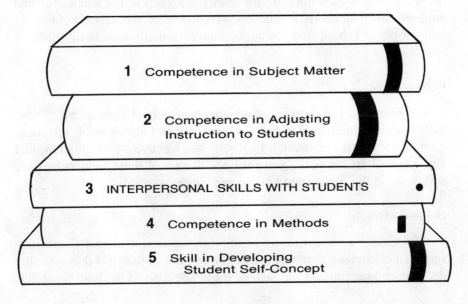

1 Competence in Subject Matter

2 Competence in Adjusting Instruction to Students

3 INTERPERSONAL SKILLS WITH STUDENTS

4 Competence in Methods

5 Skill in Developing Student Self-Concept

percent of the principals indicated that about three-fourths of their teachers have either one preparation per day or four or more preparations per day. Forty-nine percent of the schools reported that 25 percent of the teachers have one preparation per day. Unfortunately, 38 percent also reported that up to one-fourth of their teachers have four or more preparations per day.

Supervision of the Instructional Staff

Principals were asked to indicate those subject areas in which full-time supervisors were available to teachers (Table 3.8A). About one-third of the schools have full-time subject supervisors available in most subject areas. The highest percentages were reported in English/language arts (39 percent), mathematics and social science (36 percent), and science and vocational education (35 percent).

Male to Female Ratio

Principals were asked about the percentage of full-time male teachers as the basis for determining male to female ratios in the schools. These data are also available for 1965 and 1977. The ratio of males to females is declining after being relatively stable from 1965 to 1977. Table 3.9A shows that 49 percent of the schools now report teaching staffs in which males make up less than half. In both 1965 and 1977, only 36 percent of the schools so reported.

Homeroom Teacher Responsibilities

Homeroom teacher responsibilities were the basis for a new survey question. The homeroom does not exist in 40 percent of the schools surveyed, and is used only for attendance purposes or for attendance and administrative functions in another 48 percent of the schools. Only 11 percent of the schools use the homeroom for an advisement or guidance function.

CURRICULUM

A number of influences affect the high school curriculum. These include groups interested in content, textbook and library book selection, grouping practices, graduation requirements, electives, accreditation, and level-to-level articulation. Questions about each of these influences were addressed in the survey and are reported in this section.

Influence Groups

Principals were asked to identify the groups that most influence selection of content, textbooks, and library books. Teachers dominate the decision-making process for each of these selection tasks, with principals and district supervisors next in influence, but ranking well below teachers (Table 3.10A).

Principals were also asked if they had standing curriculum committees at the building level. Sixty-one percent of the schools reported having such a committee.

Graduation Requirements and Electives

Principals reported several changes in graduation requirements. The number of credit hours required for graduation increased in mathematics, science, computer skills, and language arts. Some decreases occurred in physical education, home economics, vocational education, and business education (Table 3.11A). The impact of the changes was greatest in mathematics, science, computer skills, and business education.

The number of credit hours of electives that a student may choose to meet minimum graduation requirements is shown in Table 3.12A. The number of these credit hours increased in 35 percent of the schools reporting and decreased in 47 percent.

Accreditation and Articulation

Both accreditation and level-to-level articulation exert some influence on the high school curriculum. Eighty-one percent of the schools reporting indicated that they are accredited by a regional accrediting agency; 19 percent are not.

Principals expressed satisfaction/dissatisfaction with five features of articulation at either elementary/middle school or college levels. Generally, principals are satisfied with articulation practices. Some dissatisfaction with elementary/middle school articulation centered on counseling services and subject content and sequence (22 and 19 percent, respectively). Dissatisfaction with college articulation focused on the same areas but at lower levels (9 and 12 percent, respectively).

PROGRAM FEATURES

Program features addressed in the survey include forms of student grouping, provisions for gifted and talented, alternative and community-based programs, and advanced technology. Principals' opinions were elicited on basic skills attainment, and promotion and graduation policies.

Student Grouping Practices

Fifty-four percent of the schools sampled reported no use of formal ability grouping. Of the remaining schools, 45 percent reported grouping in college preparatory courses, 35 percent in general courses, and 20 percent in vocational education courses (Table 3.13A).

31

Those principals who reported formal ability grouping were also asked to indicate how students were assigned to classes. Student interest or choice was cited first, followed by teacher recommendation. Standardized tests are used most frequently for grouping in mathematics, language arts, and science, with 40, 36, and 27 percent of the schools reporting the practice (Table 3.14A). In a related question, only 24 percent of the schools surveyed had classes of two or more periods in which two or more subjects were combined or correlated (i.e. core, general education, humanities, etc.)

Gifted and Talented Programs

The percentages of schools offering a given type of program for gifted and talented students are shown in Table 3.15. Twenty-seven percent of the schools reported no formal program for the gifted and talented. Individualized projects are used by 31 percent of the schools. Twenty-seven percent reported separate, full-time programs. An additional 20 percent have released time or pull-out programs and 22 percent have a cooperative program with a college or university.

For those schools reporting gifted and talented programs, principals were asked to indicate practices used for admission and retention of students in the programs. (Seventy-three percent of the schools reporting have formal programs.) Teacher nomination or recommendation is the primary basis for admission to these programs (61 percent). Students are dropped most often because of grades (Table 3.16A).

Alternative Programs

The percentages of schools offering various alternative programs, including Advanced Placement, are given in Table 3.17. Seventy-eight percent of the schools reported offering college-level (AP) courses. Sixty-eight percent provide summer school enrichment or remedial programs and

TABLE 3.15
Types of Gifted/Talented Programs

Program Type	
No gifted/talented program	27
Regular classes with individualized projects for the gifted/talented	31
Full-time program	27
Cooperative program with college or university	22
Released time during school hours (special class or "pull-out program")	20
Internship/mentor program	16
After school, evening, or weekend program	11
Resource rooms	10
Other	9
Program offered in conjunction with district, region, or state department of education	7
Summer program	6
Specialized school in district	4

TABLE 3.17
Types of Alternative Programs

Programs	1987	1977
College-level courses	78	68
Summer school enrichment or remediation programs	68	78
Off-campus work experience	60	61
Credit by contract or independent study	50	54
Credit by examination	27	17
Community volunteer programs	24	17
Other	4	4

off-campus work experience. The availability of alternative programs has generally increased since 1977, with the exception of summer school, which has declined by 10 percentage points.

Community-Based Programs

Data on participation in community-based programs are given in Table 3.18A. Seventy-nine percent of the schools in the sample reported a student participation rate below 20 percent. Fifteen percent reported a rate between 20 and 40 percent.

Computer Technology

Principals were asked to indicate the various ways that computers, data processing, and other technological services were used in their schools (Table 3.19). Most of the highly ranked alternatives are administrative (e.g., scheduling and grade reporting at 71 percent each; attendance at 66 percent). Five uses related directly to instruction: library and media center operations, 53 percent; assisting teachers in developing tests, 34 percent; scoring teacher-made tests, 38 percent; identifying and retrieving materials for instruction, 13 percent; and interactive communication with other professionals, 7 percent.

Principals were also asked to estimate the promise of technological advances for improving instruction. Eighty-six percent believe that technological advances have some to considerable promise for this purpose.

PRINCIPALS' VIEWS

Principals were asked their opinions about educational purposes, formal checks of basic skills' attainment, individualized promotion, and graduation decisions.

Educational Purposes

Principals were asked to rank a set of statements about the educational purposes of schools. The list was identical to that used in the 1977 survey, which in turn had three additions to the original 1965 list. Acquisition of

TABLE 3.19
Computer Technology Uses

Computer Uses	
To schedule classes	71
To prepare grade reports	71
To maintain student records on attendance	66
To maintain fiscal records	58
As part of library media center operations of the school	53
As basic equipment for office personnel	51
To prepare written communications such as brochures, newsletters, etc.	48
To score teacher-made tests	38
To assist teachers in developing tests	34
To maintain personal records	26
To maintain student records on disciplinary behaviors	21
To select samples for student surveys	19
To provide computer-based telephone messages to the home (e.g., to notify of student absences)	15
To select samples for surveys of parents and citizens	13
As an interactive communication device to identify and retrieve materials for instruction	13
As an interactive communication device with other professionals	7
To provide a "hot-line" information service for persons who call the school	2

basic skills, development of self-concept, and development of critical inquiry and problem-solving skills remain ranked one, two, and three respectively. The other rankings generally are similar to those of 1977, with three exceptions. Preparation for a changing world moved to fourth rank from eighth; knowledge and skills in preparation for family life moved to ninth from sixth; and development of skills to operate a technological society moved from tenth to eighth. Various shifts were more pronounced from 1965 to 1977 (Table 3.20).

Basic Skills' Attainment

Forty-eight percent of the principals surveyed favor formal checks of basic skills' attainment. An additional 20 percent not only favor them but have a system in place for doing these checks.

Promotion and Graduation Practices

Thirty-nine percent of the principals favor individualized promotion; an additional 6 percent have a system for it. Thirty-three percent are undecided and 18 percent are opposed to the concept. Principals were also asked about six practices employed in making promotion and graduation decisions—whether the school had such a practice and what their own personal preferences were. Competency tests and minimum grade point averages were most frequently cited, but only in 25 and 22 percent of the schools surveyed. Mastery tests were most preferred for promotion (26 percent) and competency tests for graduation (25 percent).

TABLE 3.20
Principals' Beliefs About Educational Purposes

Educational Purposes	Rank 1987	Rank 1977	Rank 1965
Acquisition of basic skills (reading, writing, computing)	1	1	1
Development of positive self-concept (and good human relations)	2	2	7
Development of skills and practice of critical intellectual inquiry and problem solving	3	3	4
Preparation for a changing world	4	8	5
Development of moral and spiritual values	5	4	2
Career planning and training in specific entry level occupational skills	6	5	–
Understanding of the American value system (political, economic, social)	7	7	3
Development of skills to operate a technological society (engineering, scientific)	8	10	8
Knowledge about and skills in preparation for family life	9	6	–
Physical fitness and useful leisure time sports	10	9	6
Appreciation for and experience with the fine arts	11	11	–

TABLE 3.21
Promotion and Graduation Practices

Practices	In Use Promotion	In Use Graduation	Principals' Preferences Promotion	Principals' Preferences Graduation
Standardized tests—local	16	10	16	12
Mastery tests	19	13	26	18
Competency tests	12	28	20	25
Standardized tests—state	12	14	10	9
Comprehensive exit exam	7	11	8	20
Minimum grade point average	22	25	14	20
Other:	18	21	9	10

Educational Initiatives

Principals were asked about their personal involvement in school initiatives on instruction, the instructional staff, students and student relations, administration, parent/community relations, and innovative programs. These data show a somewhat mixed response, but 50 percent or more indicate "strong new initiatives" or "moderate new initiatives" for each item. Supervision and evaluation of the instructional staff are the most frequently mentioned of the established programs. The strongest new initiatives are steps to enhance instructional standards and expectations, and various innovative programs (Table 3.22A).

35

Summary

Expenditure per student roughly doubled between 1977 and 1987. Important gains also were made in average daily attendance, retention rate, and percent of students entering college.

Principals believe that the most important teacher skills and characteristics are competence in subject matter, competence in adjusting instruction to varying needs of students, interpersonal skills in working with students, competence in methods of instruction, and skill in developing positive student self-concept. The male to female ratio of teachers continued to decline during the past two decades. In 1987, 49 percent of the schools reported that the percentage of males was less than half of the teaching faculty.

Teachers are the most important influence in subject content, textbook, and library book selection. Graduation requirements have increased in mathematics, science, computer skills, and English/language arts. Ability grouping was reported in about half the high schools surveyed and 73 percent of the schools had some form of special provisions for the gifted and talented. Computer technology continues to make gains for administrative and instructional uses.

Ranking of educational purposes revealed minor changes between 1977 and 1987. (Significant shifts occurred between 1965 and 1977.) Acquisition of basic skills, positive self-concept, and skills in critical inquiry and problem solving continue to be ranked first, second, and third. More than half the principals reported strong or moderate involvement in creating new educational initiatives. They also reported wide variety in promotion and graduation practices.

IV The Assistant Principalship

T he secondary school principalship, as conceptualized in this study, is not embodied in a single person or even in a list of tasks on a position description. In broad terms, the principalship encompasses all the tasks and all the persons involved in organizing and administering a school. The assistant principal (AP) as a person and the assistant principalship as a role are integral parts of the principalship. A major thrust of this study has been to determine how the assistant principalship functions in relation to the principalship. What do assistant principals do? How important is what they do to the efficient and effective functioning of schools? How much freedom and responsibility do assistant principals have for doing what they do? How has the role of the assistant principal changed over the years? These and other questions about the assistant principalship are the focus of this chapter.

DUTIES AND RESPONSIBILITIES OF ASSISTANT PRINCIPALS

In the 1987 national survey, both principals and assistant principals were asked to respond to a comprehensive question about the duties and responsibilities of assistant principals. Respondents were asked to review 65 duties traditionally delegated to assistant principals and to indicate 1) the degree of responsibility assistant principals had for each duty, 2) how important the duty was to the proper functioning of the school, and 3) the level of discretionary behavior involved in performing the duty. The duties were grouped for convenience into the following categories: school management, staff personnel, community relations, curriculum and instruction, student activities, and student services.

A similar question was included in the 1965 NASSP Study of the Secondary-School Principalship and reported in the 1970 volume on *The Assistant Principalship*. The 1965 survey proposed 59 duties in six categories for evaluation by respondents. The same six categories were used for grouping the duties of assistant principals in the 1987 survey except that "pupil personnel" was renamed "student services." Fifty-eight of the original 59 duties from the 1965 survey were retained. (Only "field trips" was omitted.) But seven duties were added to the 1987 survey: instructional methods, instructional software, computer services, staff inservice, graduation activities, teacher incentives/motivation, and special education (IEPs).

Respondents were asked to indicate the degree of responsibility assistant principals had for each delegated administrative duty by marking one of four choices: "not applicable," "slight," "shared," or "full." If a respondent marked "not applicable," the assistant principal was assumed not to have responsibility for that particular duty. "Slight" responsibility was defined as "the principal does the job and assistant principals may aid at his discretion." "Shared" meant the duty was "delegated with close supervision; the principal and assistant principals work together." "Full" responsibility meant a duty was "delegated with general supervision; assistant principals are held responsible for the job."

Survey respondents were asked to assess the importance of each delegated duty to the proper functioning of the school by choosing one of the following: "least," "minor," "average," "major," or "most." And finally, respondents judged the level of discretionary behavior involved in the completion of a delegated duty as either "high" or "low." "High" was defined as "behavior that is self-directing, involving high-order decision making," while "low" meant "behavior that is directed in large measure by others; behavior that involves restricted high-order decision making."

It should be noted that when respondents selected "not applicable" for a particular duty, they did not generally make a judgment about the importance of the duty to the proper functioning of the school, or the level of discretionary behavior assistant principals had for carrying out the duty. For this reason, the total responses reflected in the table for degree of responsibility and level of discretionary behavior may be less than 100 percent.

Duties Delegated to Assistant Principals

Any discussion of the duties performed by assistant principals should perhaps begin with a few words about who decides what those duties will be. Both principals and assistant principals who responded to the survey were asked to select from a list of 11 possibilities, the person or persons who assigned the duties and responsibilities of assistant principals. The most frequent responses were "the principal in conference with assistant principal," (chosen by 37 percent of the APs and 34 percent of the principals), and the "principal alone," (with 29 percent of the APs and 28 percent of the principals). Sixteen percent of the principals and nine percent of the assistant principals said the duties and responsibilities of assistant principals were determined by the "principal in conference with superintendent and assistant principal." Six percent of the principals and 9 percent of the assistants added the "school board" to the decision-making group. If all responses are considered, the assistant principal is consulted about his or her job duties somewhat more than half the time.

An important task facing the research team was how to organize the considerable amount of survey data so that a profile of the duties and responsibilities of assistant principals could be produced, and the results compared in a meaningful way with the results of the 1965 study. The research team decided that assistant principals' perceptions of the level of responsibility for each duty in the survey were the most suitable criteria for organizing the discussion. For example, if assistant principals perceived that they had little or no responsibility for a particular duty, then the importance of that duty to the proper functioning of the school took on less importance in our understanding of the role of the assistant principal.

The responses of assistant principals to the degree of responsibility for each of the 65 delegated duties are grouped systematically. Responses of "not applicable" and "slight" and those of "shared" and "full" are combined. Delegated duties for which more than 50 percent of the assistant principals said they had either "shared" or "full" responsibility are considered important for understanding the role of the assistant principal in the functioning principalship. These duties are the subject of the discussion that follows. The remainder of the delegated duties, those receiving less than 50 percent support, are construed as less important in understanding the role of the assistant principal and are not discussed further.

Thirty duties remain after the 50 percent responsibility criterion has been applied to the 65 duties in the survey. Grouped by area, these 30 duties include 8 under school management, 6 under staff/personnel, 6 for curriculum and instruction, 4 for community relations, 3 for student activities, and 3 for student services. The 30 duties are as follows:

School Management: A classification encompassing the day-to-day practical tasks of organizing and running the school and providing operational resources for the educational program.

- School policies
- Special arrangements at start and close of school year
- Graduation activities
- Emergency arrangements
- Building use—school-related
- School calendars
- Daily school bulletins
- Clerical services

Staff/Personnel: Duties relating directly to securing and maintaining the human resources necessary to carry out the school's program.

- Teacher "duty" rosters
- Orientation program for new teachers
- Faculty meetings
- Substitute teachers
- Teacher selection
- Teacher incentives, motivation

Curriculum and Instruction: Activities linked to the courses of study and instruction offered by the school, the improvement of instruction through supervision of the instructional staff, the revision of curricula, and staff inservice.

- Teacher evaluation
- School master schedule
- Instructional methods
- Curriculum development
- Staff inservice
- Innovations, experiments, and research

Community Relations: Duties associated with giving and receiving information about the school and its programs, and about students and staff.

- Administrative representation at community functions
- School public relations program
- Liaison with community youth-serving agencies

Student Activities: Responsibility for the non-classroom activities of students.

- Assemblies
- School dances
- School club programs

Student Services: Duties associated with student problems and concerns, and with their personal and physical well-being.

- Student discipline
- Student attendance
- Orientation program for new students

Variety is clearly an important job characteristic in the assistant principalship. The data indicate that assistant principals have shared or full responsibility for a wide range of duties in a typical high school. Table 4.1 presents a ranking of delegated administrative duties by degree of responsibility as perceived by assistant principals in both the 1987 and 1965 studies.

For comparison, the same responsibility criterion (more than 50 percent of assistant principals reporting "shared" or "full" responsibility for a particular duty) was applied to the data of the 1965 study. Ranking of 1965 duties with identical totals was determined by the higher percentage in the "slight" category. Application of this criterion yielded a total of 28 duties in 1965, compared with the 30 duties in the 1987 survey. Twenty-five duties met the responsibility criterion in both the 1965 and 1987 studies. Three duties, "articulation with feeder schools," "school guidance program," and "providing instructional materials" met the criterion in 1965, but not in 1987. One duty, "teacher selection," met the criterion in 1987, but not in 1965. Four duties meeting the criterion in 1987 did not appear on the 1965

TABLE 4.1
Assistant Principals' Ratings of Their Administrative Duties
for Degree of Responsibility

Duties	1987		1965	
	Rank	%*	Rank	%
Student Discipline	1	88	1	90
School Policies	2	83	5	76
Evaluation of Teachers	3	82	23	55
Special Arrangements	4	82	2	89
Student Attendance	5	81	3	82
Graduation Activities	6	75	**	**
Emergency Arrangements	7	74	4	79
Building Use—School Related	8	70	24	54
Orientation Program for New Students	9	70	11	63
Assemblies	10	66	12	63
Teacher "Duty" Rosters	11	65	8	71
Administrative Representative	12	64	13	62
School Master Schedule	13	63	14	61
School Dances	14	63	9	71
Instructional Methods	15	62	**	**
Orientation Programs for New Teachers	16	61	6	73
Faculty Meetings	17	58	10	69
Substitute Teachers	18	58	26	53
School Calendars	19	57	17	58
Curriculum Development	20	56	21	56
School Daily Bulletins	21	56	15	61
Clerical Services	22	56	20	56
Staff Inservice	23	55	**	**
Teacher Selection	24	54	37	36
Teacher Incentives, Motivation	25	54	**	**
School Public Relations Program	26	53	7	71
School Club Program	27	53	18	58
Liaison with Youth-Serving Agencies	28	53	22	56
Informing Public of School Achievements	29	52	25	54
Innovations, Experiments, Research	30	51	27	53
School Guidance Program	33	47	19	57
Articulation with Feeder Schools	39	42	16	59
Instructional Media and Materials	43	38	28	50

*Total of "shared" plus "full" responsibility
** Task not on 1965 survey

survey: "graduation activities," "instructional methods," "staff inservice," and "teacher incentives/motivation." In all, a total of 33 duties met the responsibility criterion in one or both studies.

A superficial inspection of Table 4.1 might suggest that assistant principals' perceptions of responsibility for particular duties have changed very little during the 22 years that have intervened between the two studies. Four of the top 5, 5 of the top 7, 12 of the top 20, and 25 of the top 30 duties remained in the same relative positions in both studies. "Student discipline," which ranked first both in 1965 and 1987, "school policies," "special arrangements at start and close of school year," "student attendance," and "emergency arrangements" were typical duties for most assistant principals between 1965 and 1987. More than 70 percent of the assistant principals

41

who responded to the surveys said they had "full" or "shared" responsibility for these duties.

Some rather significant shifts occurred, however, in how assistant principals perceived responsibility for several duties. "Evaluation of teachers" moved from twenty-third place in the 1965 survey to third in the 1987 survey. "School-related building use" moved from twenty-fourth place in 1965 to eighth in 1987. "Teacher selection" did not meet the responsibility criterion in 1965 but ranked twenty-fourth in 1987. "Graduation activities," "instructional methods," "staff inservice," and "teacher incentives/motivation," did not appear on the 1965 survey, but were ranked in the top 25 in 1987.

At the other end of the spectrum, assistant principals in 1987 believed that they had less responsibility for certain administrative duties than their counterparts in 1965. "School public relations" dropped from seventh place in 1965 to twenty-sixth in 1987, while "orientation programs for new teachers" fell from sixth to sixteenth place. Three duties that placed in the top 28 in the 1965 study did not make the top 30 in the 1987 study: "articulation with feeder schools," "school guidance program," and "providing instructional materials."

Thus far the discussion has focused on the perceptions of assistant principals. A great amount of data was also gathered about principals' perceptions of assistant principals' administrative duties in the school. Tables 4.2 through 4.7 present a comparison of principals' and assistant principals' perceptions of delegated administrative duties in 1965 and 1987.

Several generalizations seem justified from the data in Table 4.2. First, principals in the 1987 survey perceive assistant principals as having considerably less responsibility for school management duties than assistant

TABLE 4.2
Principals' and Assistant Principals' Perceptions of Assistant Principals'
Responsibility for School Management Duties

| | As seen by the Assistant Principal | | | | | | As seen by the Principal | | | | | |
| | 1987 | | | 1965 | | | 1987 | | | 1965 | | |
	Shared	Full	Total	Shared	Full	Total	Shared	Full	Total	Shared	Full	Total
School policies*	80	3	83	75	1	76	62	6	68	75	3	78
Special arrangements	73	9	82	80	9	89	58	10	68	78	10	88
Graduation activities	61	14	75	**	**	**	44	16	60	**	**	**
Emergency arrangements	64	10	74	57	22	79	54	9	63	59	29	88
School-related building use	48	22	70	43	11	54	38	23	61	41	16	57
School calendars	41	16	57	44	14	58	40	13	53	50	15	65
School daily bulletins	41	15	56	47	14	61	29	19	48	44	19	63
Clerical services	50	6	56	52	4	56	44	9	53	50	8	58

*1965 study included this duty under the category of staf personnel.
**Task not included on 1965 survey.

principals see themselves. Second, the perceptions of principals and assistant principals about school management duties are more consistent in the 1965 survey than in the 1987 study. Third, principals in 1965 apparently accorded more responsibility to assistant principals for school management duties than the principals of 1987. Finally, a very small proportion of both principals and assistant principals see assistant principals as having full responsibility for various school management duties.

The generalizations for school management listed above also hold true for the staff personnel duties in Table 4.3. A notable change in this category, however, is the relatively high proportion of principals and assistant principals, both in 1965 and 1987, who give full responsibility to assistant principals for "teacher duty rosters" and "substitute teachers."

Many of the earlier generalizations also apply to the data of Table 4.4, but a definite trend also emerges toward giving assistant principals more responsibility for instructional supervision. The perceptions of both principals and assistant principals in the 1987 survey about responsibility for the "evaluation of teachers" and "instructional methods" provide a striking example of assistant principals' new responsibilities in the instructional area. Another interesting development is that about 25 percent of assistant principals now have full responsibility for preparing the school master schedule.

Table 4.5 shows fairly close agreement between principals and assistants on the duties of assistant principals in community relations. The data indicate a drop since 1965 in assistant principals' responsibility in this arena, particularly for public relations. Principals also have a constrained view of the assistant principals' role as representative at community functions. Perhaps principals are personally assuming the school spokesperson role more now than in the past.

TABLE 4.3
**Principals' and Assistant Principals' Perceptions of Assistant Principals'
Responsibility for Staff/Personnel Duties**

| | As seen by the Assistant Principal | | | | | | As seen by the Principal | | | | | |
| | 1987 | | | 1965 | | | 1987 | | | 1965 | | |
	Shared	Full	Total	Shared	Full	Total	Shared	Full	Total	Shared	Full	Total
Teacher "Duty" rosters	34	31	65	46	25	71	30	30	60	44	31	75
Orientation program for new teachers	47	14	61	67	6	73	44	13	57	65	6	71
Substitute teachers	29	29	58	36	17	53	22	28	50	30	23	53
Faculty meetings	54	4	58	67	2	69	38	8	46	65	6	71
Teacher selection	52	2	54	35	2	37	47	4	51	35	1	36
Teacher incentives, motivation	52	2	54	**	**	**	47	4	51	**	**	**

**Task did not appear on 1965 survey.

TABLE 4.4
Principals' and Assistant Principals' Perceptions of Assistant Principals' Responsibility for Curriculum and Instruction Duties

| | As seen by the Assistant Principal | | | | | | As seen by the Principal | | | | | |
| | 1987 | | | 1965 | | | 1987 | | | 1965 | | |
	Shared	Full	Total	Shared	Full	Total	Shared	Full	Total	Shared	Full	Total
Evaluation of teachers	66	16	82	52	3	55	56	9	65	46	7	53
School master schedule	36	27	63	44	17	61	32	22	54	47	16	63
Instructional methods	55	7	62	**	**	**	54	5	59	**	**	**
Curriculum development	46	10	56	51	5	56	47	5	52	61	3	64
Staff inservice	49	6	55	**	**	**	46	6	52	**	**	**
Innovations, exper. and research	45	6	51	49	4	53	40	3	43	63	2	65
Articulation with feeder schools	32	10	42	51	8	59	35	7	42	55	7	62
Providing instruct. materials	30	8	38	41	9	50	34	8	42	46	10	56

**Task did not appear on the 1965 survey.

Table 4.6 indicates that assistant principals continue to have considerable responsibility for student activities. Principals generally see assistant principals as having fewer of these obligations than in 1965, but general agreement exists about current scope. Undoubtedly, assistant principals' new responsibilities in curriculum and instruction necessitate their somewhat reduced role in student activities.

Table 4.7 lists only a few areas of student service, but two are at the very top of the assistant principal's duty list. Student attendance ranked number one in both the 1987 and 1965 surveys in terms of duties for which

TABLE 4.5
Principals' and Assistant Principals' Perceptions of Assistant Principals' Responsibility for Community Relations Duties

| | As seen by the Assistant Principal | | | | | | As seen by the Principal | | | | | |
| | 1987 | | | 1965 | | | 1987 | | | 1965 | | |
	Shared	Full	Total	Shared	Full	Total	Shared	Full	Total	Shared	Full	Total
Administrative rep at comm. functions	61	3	64	60	2	62	51	4	55	63	2	65
School public relations program	48	5	53	69	2	71	46	6	52	70	4	74
Liaison with comm. youth-serving age	43	10	53	48	8	56	36	14	50	58	11	69
Informing public of school achievements	46	6	52	51	3	54	43	7	50	57	4	61

TABLE 4.6
**Principals' and Assistant Principals' Perceptions of Assistant Principals'
Responsibility for Student Activities Duties**

| | As seen by the Assistant Principal | | | | | | As seen by the Principal | | | | | |
| | 1987 | | | 1965 | | | 1987 | | | 1965 | | |
	Shared	Full	Total	Shared	Full	Total	Shared	Full	Total	Shared	Full	Total
Assemblies	46	20	66	42	21	63	40	24	64	45	28	73
School dances	45	18	63	53	18	71	39	22	61	52	27	79
School club programs	35	18	53	43	15	58	32	23	55	48	20	68

TABLE 4.7
**Principals' and Assistant Principals' Perceptions of Assistant Principals'
Responsibility for Student Services Duties**

| | As seen by the Assistant Principal | | | | | | As seen by the Principal | | | | | |
| | 1987 | | | 1965 | | | 1987 | | | 1965 | | |
	Shared	Full	Total	Shared	Full	Total	Shared	Full	Total	Shared	Full	Total
Student discipline	47	41	88	52	38	90	38	36	74	63	31	94
Student attendance	37	44	81	33	49	82	29	40	69	28	61	89
Orientation program for new students	55	15	70	51	12	63	47	15	62	56	14	70
School guidance program	37	10	47	47	10	57	31	11	42	51	10	61

assistant principals had "full" responsibility; student discipline ranked second. These rankings are reversed if "shared" or "total" responsibility data are considered. Clearly, student attendance and discipline remain primary responsibilities of the vast majority of assistant principals in American secondary schools. "Orientation programs for new students" also ranks high on the current list of assistant principals' duties.

The Perceived Importance of Duties Performed by Assistant Principals

The previous section was devoted to a discussion of the degree of responsibility assistant principals have for a range of duties and tasks in secondary schools. A knowledge of what assistant principals do is certainly a basic consideration, but perhaps even more significant is the *perceived importance* of the work performed. Are the duties and tasks performed by assistant principals critical to the proper functioning of the school, or are they perceived as rather unimportant in the total spectrum of administrative responsibility?

Survey respondents were asked to characterize each duty performed by assistant principals in terms of its level of significance to the proper functioning of the school. Respondents could choose from five degrees of importance: "least," "minor," "average," "major," and "most." Table 4.8 presents a ranking of the perceptions of assistant principals on the degree of importance of their delegated duties. The table includes the 33 duties for which assistant principals have either "shared" or "full" responsibility, as perceived by more than 50 percent of the assistant principals responding to either the 1965 or the 1987 surveys.

The rankings in Table 4.8 were determined by totaling the percentages of "major" and "most" responses for each individual duty. If two or more

TABLE 4.8
**Assistant Principals' Ratings of Their Administrative Duties
for Degree of Importance**

Duties	1987		1965	
	Rank	%	Rank	%
Student Discipline	1	82	1	83
Evaluation of Teachers	2	80	7	64
School Policies	3	71	4	69
Student Attendance	4	71	2	76
School Master Schedule	5	67	3	72
Curriculum Development	6	63	5	67
Teacher Selection	7	61	6	67
Instructional Methods	8	55	**	**
Special Arrangements at Start and Close of School Year	9	52	10	55
Graduation Activities	10	49	**	**
Informing the Public of School Achievements	11	47	19	37
Emergency Arrangements	12	46	11	54
Orientation Program for New Teachers	13	44	8	62
Orientation Program for New Students	14	42	15	44
Teacher Incentives Motivation	15	42	**	**
Building Use—School Related	16	41	26	20
School Public Relations Program	17	41	13	48
Administrative Rep. at Community Functions	18	40	23	29
Staff Inservice	19	38	**	**
School Calendars	20	37	21	37
Faculty Meetings	21	36	16	43
Substitute Teachers	22	36	22	37
Teacher "Duty" Rosters	23	36	18	38
Clerical Services	24	33	20	37
Liaison with Community Youth-Serving Agencies	25	26	22	30
School-Daily Bulletins	26	25	24	27
Innovations, Experiments and Research	27	25	17	42
Assemblies	28	24	27	19
School Club Program	29	23	25	23
School Dances	30	15	28	17
Articulation with Feeder Schools	*		14	48
School Guidance Program	*		9	62
Instructional Media and Materials	*		12	52

*These duties did not meet the criterion for responsibility in 1987.
**These duties were not included on the 1965 survey.

duties had equal percentages of "major" and "most" responses, then the duty with the higher percentage of "average" responses was given the higher ranking.

Student discipline, which is ranked first, was rated by 82 percent of the assistant principals who responded to the 1987 survey as of "major" or "most" importance. (Eighty-three percent of the assistant principals rated it similarly in the 1965 survey.)

Table 4.8 shows that assistant principals believe that many of their duties are very important to the proper functioning of the school. "Student discipline" and "evaluation of teachers" were clearly perceived as the most important duties performed by assistant principals. "School policies," "student attendance," "school master schedule," "curriculum development," "teacher selection," "instructional methods," and "special arrangements at start and close of school year" were also judged to be of "major" or "most" importance by more than 50 percent of the assistant principals responding to the survey.

For the most part, assistant principals in both the 1965 and 1987 surveys agreed; the top six duties in terms of importance, slightly reshuffled, remain the same in both surveys. The other duties ranked in the top 10 of the 1987 survey ("instructional methods" and "graduation activities") were not included in the 1965 survey. "Special arrangements at the start and close of school year" is ranked ninth in both surveys.

Apparently a close relationship exists between the degree of responsibility assistant principals have for administrative duties and the perceived importance of those duties. Assistant principals responding to the 1987 survey ranked "student discipline," "school policies," and "evaluation of teachers" as the top three both in terms of degree of responsibility and in perceived importance to the proper functioning of the school. Table 4.9 delineates this close relationship.

In general, principals who participated in the survey agreed with assistant principals about the importance of delegated duties to the proper functioning of the school. Where significant disagreement emerged, principals tended to regard specific duties as less important than did assistant principals. Only 4 of the 65 duties listed in the survey showed a difference of 10 percentage points or more: "evaluation of teachers," "school master schedule," "school policies," and "student discipline."

Discretionary Behavior in Duties Performed by Assistant Principals

The discussion thus far has addressed the delegated duties of assistant principals and their importance to the functioning of the school. We now turn our attention to the third variable, the level of discretionary behavior in duties that are delegated to assistant principals. Do assistant principals have freedom to make decisions in delegated areas of responsibility, or are they largely dependent on others to make decisions for them?

TABLE 4.9
Assistant Principals' Rating of Their Administrative Duties
for Degree of Responsibility and Degree of Importance

	Rank by Responsibility	Rank by Degree of Importance
Student Discipline	1	1
School Policies	2	3
Evaluation of Teachers	3	2
Special Arrangements	4	9
Student Attendance	5	4
Graduation Activities	6	10
Emergency Arrangements	7	12
Building—School Related	8	16
Operation Program for New Students	9	14
Assemblies	10	28
Teacher "Duty" Rosters	11	23
Administrative Representative at Community Functions	12	18
School Master Schedule	13	5
School Dances	14	30
Instructional Methods	15	8

Survey participants were asked to judge the degrees of freedom assistant principals had in carrying out delegated administrative duties. Respondents could choose either "low" or "high." "Low" discretionary behavior was defined as "behavior that is directed in large measure by others; behavior that involves restricted high-order decision making." "High" discretionary behavior was defined as "behavior that is self-directing, involving high-order decision making."

Table 4.10 presents a ranking of the perceptions of assistant principals about the levels of discretionary behavior in their administrative responsibilities. The table includes the 30 duties for which assistant principals have either "shared" or "full" responsibility as perceived by more than 50 percent of the assistant principals in the 1987 survey.

The rankings in Table 4.10 are based on the percentage of assistant principals who indicated that a "high" level of discretionary behavior was involved in carrying out a particular duty. For example, 77 percent of the assistant principals rated "student discipline" (ranked first) as "high" in level of discretionary behavior, compared to 89 percent for the 1965 survey.

Table 4.10 shows that assistant principals see themselves as having considerable discretion in carrying out the administrative duties delegated to them. In 10 areas of responsibility, at least 50 percent of the assistant principals in the 1987 survey indicated that they exercised a high level of discretionary behavior: "student discipline," "evaluation of teachers," "student attendance," "school policies," "special arrangements at start and close of school year," "school master schedule," "emergency arrangements," "instructional methods," "building use—school related," and "orientation program for new students."

48

TABLE 4.10
Assistant Principals' Ratings of Their Administrative Duties
for Level of Discretionary Behavior

Duties	1987		1965	
	Rank	%	Rank	%
Student Discipline	1	77	1	89
Evaluation of Teachers	2	72	3.5	67
Student Attendance	3	64	2	73
School Policies	4	59	7	63
Special Arrangements	5.5	57	3.5	67
School Master Schedule	5.5	57	5	66
Emergency Arrangements	7	53	10	60
Instructional Methods	8	52	**	**
Building Use—School Related	9	51	26	40
Orientation Program for New Students	10	50	16	51
Administrative Rep. at Community Functions	12.5	47	18	50
Informing Public of School Achievements	12.5	47	15	52
Graduation Activities	12.5	47	**	**
Orientation Program for New Teachers	12.5	47	6	65
Faculty Meetings	15	46	11	58
Substitute Teachers	17	45	22	46
Teacher Selection	17	45	13.5	54
Curriculum Development	17	45	12	55
Teacher "Duty" Rosters	19	44	8.5	61
Assemblies	20	43	25	42
School Public Relations Program	21.5	42	8.5	61
Innovations, Experiments, and Research	21.5	42	13.5	54
School Daily Bulletins	23	41	18	50
Liaison with Community Youth-Serving Agencies	25.5	38	18	50
Clerical Services	25.5	38	21	47
Teacher Incentives, Motivation	25.5	38	**	**
School Dances	25.5	38	20	48
Staff Inservice	28	37	**	**
School Calendars	29	35	23.5	45
School Club Program	30	30	23.5	45

**These duties did not appear on the 1965 survey.

The data in Table 4.10 also indicate that assistant principals in 1965 had a higher degree of discretion in performing their duties than assistant principals in 1987. In fact, assistant principals who responded to the 1987 survey reported greater discretion in only three areas: "evaluation of teachers," "building use—school related," and "assemblies."

Considerable agreement emerges among assistant principals in both surveys about the areas in which they have the most discretion. Six of the seven top ranked duties, in slightly different order, remain the same in both 1965 and 1987. The remaining duties exhibit considerable movement in the decades between the studies. The data indicate that principals generally tend to delegate authority with some constraint.

Finally, Table 4.11 points up the close relationship between the degree of responsibility assistant principals have for administrative duties and their

TABLE 4.11

Assistant Principals' Ratings of Their Administrative Duties for Degree of Responsibility and Level of Discretionary Behavior

	Rank by Responsibility	Rank by Level of Discretion
Student Discipline	1	1
School Policies	2	4
Evaluation of Teachers	3	2
Special Arrangements	4	5.5
Student Attendance	5	3
Graduation Activities	6	11.5
Emergency Arrangements	7	7
Building—School Related	8	9
Operation Program for New Students	9	10
Assemblies	10	20
Teacher "Duty" Rosters	11	19
Administrative Representative at Comm. Functions	12	11.5
School Master Schedule	13	5.5
School Dances	14	24
Instructional Methods	15	8

perceived level of discretion in carrying out those duties. The same five duties are ranked in the top five for both delegated responsibility and level of discretionary behavior.

Summary

More similarities than differences emerge when the role of the assistant principal in 1987 is compared with the role in 1965. Assistant principals have responsibility for a wide range of duties. Many traditional duties in school management and student services still remain at the heart of the assistant principalship, but the current survey showed an increased responsibility for teacher evaluation and teacher selection.

The assistant principalship is perceived by both principals and assistant principals as a very responsible position, but principals generally see assistant principals as having less responsibility for delegated duties than assistant principals do. Shared rather than full responsibility seems to be the favored mode of delegation. A close correlation exists between the level of responsibility assistant principals have for performing various duties in the school and the perceived importance of these duties to the appropriate functioning of the school.

Assistant principals also exercise considerable discretion in carrying out their major responsibilities. This freedom notwithstanding, assistant principals in 1987 reported less overall discretion for delegated duties than their counterparts did in 1965. Generally, greater divergence was found between the views of principals and assistant principals in 1987 than between their counterparts in 1965.

The assistant principal is a vital part of the school administrative team. As schools attempt to serve a more complex student population, the assistant principal may well assume an increasingly important role in the functioning principalship.

V Career Patterns of the Principalship

The 1980s have been described as "the decade of the principalship." The principalship is more than a single person or role position; yet, the individual who serves as principal has been recognized as being most responsible—for better or worse—for the quality of education provided in each school.

The principalship as conceptualized in this study includes those functions and tasks that are necessary for effective leadership in a school. Effective leadership, in turn, is defined as the ability of an individual to work with others to direct or facilitate accomplishment of meaningful goals and tasks.

Effective principals are leader-managers; i.e., they articulate a vision directed toward fulfilling individual wants and societal needs and they possess the managerial and organizational skills to convert this vision into the day-by-day reality of the school. Effective leadership and management in the principalship generally, and by the principal as a specific role position, are crucial to the future of both individual and societal growth in American schools.

One purpose of this study was to describe characteristics, conditions, and personal choices that serve to define the career patterns of high school principals. This chapter treats the educational background of principals, the first principalship, longevity in the role, career-related factors, and professional activities of principals. Since many persons serving as principals in 1987 will not be serving at the end of this century, data for individuals who first became principals in 1987 have been identified and are compared with the total sample to highlight any emerging changes in career patterns.

EDUCATIONAL BACKGROUND OF PRINCIPALS

Respondents were asked to report their major fields of study for the baccalaureate degree. A similar question was included in both the 1977 and 1965 studies. Data for 1987 are reported for new principals (i.e., first year principal in 1987) and for all principals who responded to the 1987 survey. These data, and comparative data from the 1977 and 1965 studies, are reported in Table 5.1.

In all three studies, diversity of preparation is characteristic of persons who become principals. Principals in 1965 were more likely to have a background in the humanities than principals in either 1977 or 1987, but 1987

TABLE 5.1
Undergraduate Majors of Principals

Undergraduate Major	1987 New	1987 All	1977	1965
Business	3	4	7	6
Education	11	14	12	12
Fine Arts	0	2	3	2
Humanities	11	14	12	29
Physical Education	15	16	17	11
Sciences	17	20	20	18
Social Sciences	31	24	26	14
Vocational Technical	3	4	NA	NA
Other	8	3	2	9

Notes: (1) Education includes secondary education (11%) and elementary education (3%).
(2) Sciences includes physical or biological sciences (12%) and mathematics (8%).

academic backgrounds at the baccalaureate level are strikingly similar to those of 1977. Data for new principals show an increase in social science majors.

Respondents also reported levels of formal education completed. These data, and comparable data for 1977 and 1965, are reported in Table 5.2. Two major observations can be made from these findings. First, virtually all principals (99 percent) possess at least a master's degree. Second, 38 percent in 1987 reported having a specialist or a higher academic degree, whereas the comparable figure in 1977 was 29 percent. The master's is the entry-level degree for the principalship in many states. The important trend here seems to be a higher level of preparation in 1987 than in either 1977 or 1965. This is particularly evident in the fact that 30 percent of the first-year principals who responded to the 1987 survey have degree work at or beyond the level of the educational specialist.

The First Principalship

Understanding career patterns in the principalship requires an understanding of the types of experiences possessed by those who are selected as

TABLE 5.2
Formal Education Completed by Principals

Level	1987 New	1987 All	1977	1965
Less than bachelor's degree	0	0	0	0
Bachelor's degree	0	1	1	10
Master's degree in education	30	15	12	35
Master's degree not in education	2	2	2	4
Master's degree plus additional course work	39	44	56	41
Specialist degree or equivalent	13	16	9	6
Master's degree plus all course work for doctoral degree	5	8	9	6
Doctoral degree (Ph.D. or Ed.D.)	12	13	9	1
Other	0	1	2	1

principals and of the factors that influence appointment to the job. A related demographic variable with sociological implications is the age at which individuals are selected for the first principalship. Since 1977, the average age of population in the United States and the number and percentage of the population in the older age groups have increased. We might expect a similar increase in the average age at which an individual is named to the principalship since selection of leaders often includes a subtle normative bias.

With the exception of age at first principalship, the survey questions that describe the career pattern leading to the first principalship are new to the 1987 survey and were not asked in the 1977 or 1965 surveys.

An expectation, both within the education profession and the school community, is that persons who serve as principals will have had classroom teaching experience. This expectation is reinforced by state requirements for administrator certification as well as by other societal norms. In Table 5.3, the years of teaching experience are reported for principals first appointed in 1987 as well as for all principals surveyed in this study.

No first-year principals reported fewer than three years of classroom teaching experience but 8 percent of the *total* sample reported three years or less. A requirement in administrator certification codes of a minimum of three years of classroom teaching experience may explain this trend, in part. Another possible explanation is the older age at which persons are first named to the principalship. (The age of first appointment is reported further in Table 5.6 below.)

Almost half of all first-year principals (49 percent) had 10 or more years of classroom teaching experience, and 79 percent had 7 or more. Teaching experience, *de facto* and *de jure*, is an important ingredient in the career patterns of the principalship. No meaningful differences appear in the years of teaching experience possessed by all principals surveyed and those who were first-year principals in 1987.

Although experience as a classroom teacher is characteristic of principals, only 20 percent of those surveyed in 1987 went straight from classroom teacher to the principalship. Service as an assistant principal is the most

TABLE 5.3
Years of Teaching Experience Prior to First Principalship

Years of Experience	New Principals	All Principals
None	0	0
1	0	1
2–3	0	7
4–6	21	26
7–9	30	23
10–14	28	26
15–19	8	11
20–24	8	4
25 or more	5	3

common route to the principalship. Table 5.4 shows that 54 percent of the respondents served as a high school assistant principal and 7 percent as an elementary or middle school assistant principal. Even more meaningful perhaps is the fact that persons selected as first-year principals in 1987 do not come from the elementary principalship. One possible explanation may be the level-specific nature of administrator certification codes in many states. A more likely explanation is that elementary principals who might be viable candidates are not motivated to seek high school principalships because many of the career advantages of earlier years (i.e., salary, prestige) have lessened or disappeared.

Twenty percent of those selected for the role of principal have no previous administrative experience. Service as an athletic coach (52 percent of all principals) or as a department chairperson (46 percent) are common "on-the-job" training experiences for persons who become principals. Other typical experiences include service as a guidance counselor (22 percent of all principals, 29 percent of new principals) or as an athletic director (28 percent of all principals including first-year respondents).

Persons first selected as principals in 1987 were somewhat more likely to have had prior experience as a guidance counselor than their colleagues in the general sample. Service as a guidance counselor prepares an individual to work with such problems as substance abuse, sexual abuse, and child abuse, all of which are issues of vital importance in the culture and the schools of the 1980s. Data about administrative experiences prior to the first principalship are reported in Table 5.5.

The individual's age at first appointment to the principalship has increased each decade since 1965. More than a third of all principals (35 percent) were under age 30 in 1965, but only 24 percent in 1977, and 14 percent in 1987. Of persons named to the principalship in 1987, a meager 2 percent were under age 30. Seventy-one percent of all principals surveyed in 1987 were under age 40 when first named. Fifty-one percent of those named principal in 1987 were 40 years of age or older. If these data are representative, many persons now being named to the principalship will be retiring in the next 10 to 15 years. Table 5.6 shows that selection for the role of principal now occurs at a much later age. Principals in the latter half of the

TABLE 5.4
Position Prior to First Principalship

Position	New Principals	All Principals
Teacher	20	20
Assistant Principal—Elementary or Middle School	7	4
Assistant Principal—High School	54	45
Principal— Elementary or Middle School	0	13
Guidance Counselor	2	4
Other—Education	16	13
Other—Not in Education	2	1

TABLE 5.5
Administrative Experience Prior to First Principalship

Administrative Experience	New Principals	All Principals
Athletic Coach	56	52
Athletic Director	28	28
Guidance Counselor	29	22
Dean or Registrar	13	14
Department or Area Chairperson	50	46

1980s may be "transition" leaders, providing leadership to the end of this century but being replaced by new individuals as the 21st century begins.

Data about principals' perceptions of factors influencing their selection are reported in Table 5.7. One reason this question was asked in the 1987 survey was to identify whether or not the methods and practices used for selection were changing. Of parti¹cular interest to NASSP was the question of whether or not reports from the NASSP Assessment Center or other uses of assessment center methodology were perceived as important in selection decisions.

When principals named in 1987 are compared with all principals surveyed, a number of points emerge:

- "Amount and quality of professional preparation" was ranked as important or very important by 95 percent of first-year principals but only 87 percent of the total sample.
- A "successful job interview" was ranked as important or very important by 83 percent of first-year principals and 81 percent of all principals.
- A perception that "the superintendent wanted me" was ranked as important or very important by 71 percent of both groups.

TABLE 5.6
Age at Initial Appointment to the Principalship

Age	1987		1977	1965
	New	All	New	All
Under 20*	NA	NA	0	1
23** or under	0	1	NA	NA
20–24*	NA	NA	3	9
24–29**	2	13	NA	NA
25–29*	NA	NA	19	25
30–34	21	30	28	27
35–39	26	27	24	18
40–44	26	17	15	11
45–49	18	9	7	6
50–54	7	3	3	3
55 or older	0	1	0	1

*These age groupings used only in 1977 and 1965.
**These age groupings used only in 1987.

TABLE 5.7
Factors Influencing Appointment to First Principalship

Factors	New Principals				All Principals			
	Very Important	Important	Some Importance	Little or No Importance	Very Important	Important	Some Importance	Little or No Importance
Amount and quality of professional preparation	21	75	5	0	36	51	11	2
Assessment Center report	14	14	19	52	3	11	20	66
Contacts outside the profession	0	13	30	57	4	20	23	54
Contacts within the profession	38	38	17	8	30	35	22	13
Right spot at right time	33	29	21	17	30	34	22	14
Years of teaching experience	4	60	36	0	10	35	39	16
Years of experience as an assistant principal	22	35	13	30	16	31	20	34
Performance on competitive examinations	0	4	16	80	6	4	13	77
Success as a teacher	33	33	17	17	39	30	20	11
Success as an assistant principal	50	21	4	25	52	17	4	27
Successful job interview	50	33	4	13	52	29	8	11
The superintendent wanted me	50	21	17	13	44	29	14	12

- "Success as an assistant principal" was perceived as important or very important by 71 percent of first-year principals and 69 percent of the total sample.
- First-year principals were more likely to rate contacts within the profession as important or very important (76 percent) than did the general sample (65 percent).
- First-year principals (66 percent) and all principals (69 percent) perceived "success as teacher" as an important factor in selection as a principal.
- Luck, i.e., being in the "right spot at the right time," was identified by 62 percent of first-year principals and 64 percent of all principals as an important factor.
- First-year principals were twice as likely (28 percent) to identify an "assessment center report" as an important factor in their selection as were experienced principals (14 percent). When consideration is given to the relatively small turnover in the principalship until recently and the use of assessement center reports as a phenomenon of the 1980s, identification of assessment center reports as important or very important by more than a quarter of new principals illustrates the rapid and relatively successful dissemination of this practice.

57

- Selection as a principal is perceived as the culmination of high levels of professional preparation, previous success in teaching and administration, a successful job interview, being wanted, and luck.

LONGEVITY IN THE PRINCIPALSHIP

Table 5.8 shows that persons who become principals remain in the principalship for a long time. In the 1987, 1977, and 1965 surveys, more than half the principals at any given point had served in that capacity for eight or more years; approximately two-thirds of all principals in all three surveys had served six years or more; more than 10 percent of all principals had served for 20 years. In all three surveys, the modal length of service fell in the category of 10-14 years. The principalship is a significant career role for the majority of those selected.

Data from 1987, 1977, and 1965 show that more than half of all principals have served 5 or fewer years in their *present* principalship. Table 5.9 illustrates, however, that 20 percent of the principals surveyed in 1987 have served 12 or more years in their current position. Moreover, the number of principals in 1987 who have served 15 or more years in their present position (20 percent) is appreciably higher than similar percentages for 1977 (6 percent) or 1965 (11 percent). Many of these principals with long terms of service are likely to retire within the next few years. Perhaps indicative of the growing trend to replace these individuals, the percentage of respondents in their first year of the principalship (9 percent) or in the first year of their present position (15 percent) is considerably higher than comparable figures for 1977.

CAREER MOVEMENT, SATISFACTION, AND ASPIRATIONS

Table 5.10 reports data that were collected in 1987 but not in the earlier surveys. Principals were asked to identify factors that influenced their decisions to move from one school district to another. First-year principals were somewhat less likely to list family commitment and somewhat more likely to list job security as important factors. They were also more likely to

TABLE 5.8
Years in the Principalship

Years	1987	1977	1965
1	9	5	8
2–3	14	14	14
4–5	10	15	13
6–7	13	12	11
8–9	10	11	10
10–14	22	21	18
15–19	12	11	10
20–24	8	6	6
25 or more	3	4	9

TABLE 5.9
Years as Principal in Present Position

Years	1987	1977	1965
1	15	12	16
2	13	13	14
3	10	11	12
4–5	15	19	18
6–8	17	21	15
9–11	11	11	9
12–14	8	6	5
15–17	6	NA	NA
15 or more	12	6	11
18 or more	6	NA	NA

Note: 1987 data for 15–17 years and 18 or more years are combined to permit comparison with 15 or more years in 1977 and 1965.

describe the school environment in a bipolar manner, i.e., 68 percent described the context of the school as "important," while 24 percent saw it as of little or no importance. In general, the pattern of responses for the first-year principals and the general sample is comparable for this question.

Data from the 1977 and 1987 surveys support the conclusion that schools with smaller student populations have younger principals, and schools with larger student populations have older principals. Age (and in all likelihood longevity in the principalship) and size of student population are related in a predictable manner.

Eighty-one percent of the principals in the 1987 survey are 40 or older, but 96 percent of the principals in schools with student enrollments of 2,000 or more are 40 or older. Eighty-two percent of the principals under 40 years of age are working in schools with enrollments of fewer than 1,000 students. Fifty-eight percent of the principals in large schools with more than 2,000 students are 50 years of age or older, but only 35 percent of the principals in the current survey are that age.

TABLE 5.10
Factors Influencing Career Movement

Factors	New Principals			All Principals		
	Important	Moderate Importance	Little or No Importance	Important	Moderate Importance	Little or No Importance
Family commitments	42	21	38	49	21	30
Location—more place-oriented than career-oriented	35	35	30	39	36	25
School environment, i.e., student discipline, parental view on education	68	8	24	64	26	10
Job security, e.g., seniority and retirement benefits	48	32	20	30	42	27

59

TABLE 5.11
Age of Principals by School Size

Age	1987 Enrollment			1977 Enrollment		
	0-999	1,000–1,999	2,000 or more	0-999	1,000–1,999	2,000 or more
20–39	83	16	2	68	28	4
40–49	65	27	8	52	34	14
50 or older	43	40	16	42	40	18

Principals' satisfaction with their choice of career was investigated in 1965, 1977, and 1987. Table 5.12 indicates that during the past 22 years, principals report a slow but steady increase in reported levels of satisfaction with career choice. In 1987, 72 percent of all principals reported that they "definitely" or "probably" would make the same career choice. Sixty-nine percent gave that response in 1977, and only 50 percent in 1965. In both 1987 and 1977, 15 percent indicated that they were "uncertain" about the same career choice again; in 1965, the figure was 22 percent.

Although their response may be attributable to a "Hawthorne" effect, first-year principals in the 1987 study were more positive about the principalship as a career choice (79 percent) than the general sample (72 percent).

Questions about the career aspirations of principals were included in the 1987, 1977, and 1965 studies. Response choices for the 1987 study were different in many respects from questions asked in earlier studies. Thus, direct comparisons across the three studies are problematic. More than 40 percent of the current sample would remain in the same position. Somewhat fewer principals in 1987 would seek a superintendency or central office position (27 percent) than in 1977 (33 percent), but considerably more than in 1965 (14 percent). The number of those undecided about future plans has dropped noticeably, from 25 percent in 1965 to 9 percent in 1987. Principals today are more likely to perceive the principalship as a career goal or a defined step on a career ladder than in earlier years.

Data in Table 5.13 show that 90 percent of the 1987 respondents expect to make one or four career choices:

1. Remain in their present position as principal (41 percent)

2. Seek a position as a superintendent (15 percent)

TABLE 5.12
Satisfaction of Principals with Career Choice

Would Principal Make the Same Career Choice	1987 New	1987 All	1977	1965
Definitely yes	54	43	37	60
Probably yes	25	29	32	NA
Uncertain	17	15	15	22
Probably not	4	11	12	NA
Definitely not	0	3	3	17

TABLE 5.13
Career Aspirations of Principals

Career Aspirations	1987 New	All	1977	1965
Remain in present position	44	41	NA	NA
Retirement	12	14	NA	NA
Seek a position as superintendent	24	15	NA	NA
Seek a central office position other than the superintendency	0	12	NA	NA
Seek a different position as a high school principal	8	5	NA	NA
Seek a position as an elementary or middle level school principal	4	2	NA	NA
Seek a position in a junior/community college or university	0	1	5	5
Seek a position in a state department of education or other type of educational service agency	0	0	NA	NA
Return to full-time teaching	0	0	5	10
Seek a position in a career field other than education	0	2	NA	NA
Principalship in a larger district	NA	NA	4	12
Principalship in a smaller district	NA	NA	0	0
Superintendency or central office position	NA	NA	33	14
Some other position	NA	NA	5	10
Undecided	8	9	20	25
No Response	NA	NA	28	28

Note: Data from 1977 and 1965 surveys reported in the categories used for 1987 survey, whenever possible.

3. Retire (14 percent), or

4. Seek a central office position other than the superintendency (12 percent).

Earlier in this report we noted that the elementary principalship is not a career route to the secondary principalship. The reverse is also true. Only 2 percent of the principals surveyed anticipated a possible career move to either an elementary or middle school principalship. First-year principals were more likely to consider such a move (4 percent) than their colleagues. A related item of interest is the intention of 12 percent of the new principals to retire within the next three to five years.

One very disturbing finding in the current survey is the virtual absence (1 percent) of career aspirations for postsecondary positions. A concern for the profession, during this and the next decade, will be the next generation of professors who direct principal preparation programs.

PROFESSIONAL ACTIVITIES

The range and nature of professional activities required of, or available to principals has increased dramatically. When the 1987 study was designed, many questions asked in 1977 were not adequate to permit description of the

61

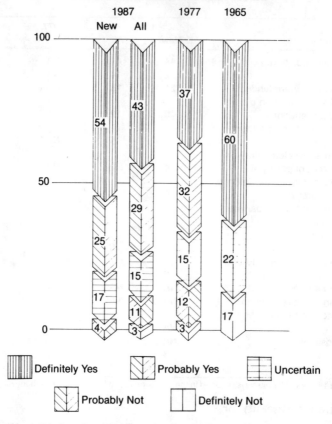

FIGURE E (BASED ON TABLE 5.12)
Satisfaction of Principals with Career Choice

Definitely Yes Probably Yes Uncertain

Probably Not Definitely Not

range of professional activities that occupy principals in the 1980s; e.g., voluntary participation in principal centers or academies. Data from the 1987 and 1977 studies are reported in Table 5.14. (The 1965 survey lacked a question about professional activities.) In both studies, respondents were asked to identify their professional activities during the two years preceding the survey.

Despite the differences in response choices, some comparisons of the findings can be made.

- In 1977, attendance at national meetings of the NASSP or other educational organizations was reported by 57 percent of the respondents; in 1987, attendance at national organization institutes or conferences was cited by 54 percent of the respondents. These figures, in all likelihood, do not accurately depict the actual changes that have occurred. The number of institutes, workshops, academies, and professional activities other than the annual convention of professional organizations has increased notably since 1977. In 1977, a "national meeting" often meant only the national convention. This is less true in 1987.
- In 1977, enrollment in institutions of higher education was reported by 38 percent of the respondents; in 1987, the comparable figure was

62

TABLE 5.14
Professional Activities of Principals

Professional Activities During Past Two Years	1987 New	1987 All	1977
National professional organization institute or conference (voluntary participation)	38	54	NA
State professional organization activity (voluntary participation)	75	73	NA
Activity conducted by private consultants at an out-of-district location (voluntary participation)	38	45	NA
District activity required as part of employment	63	69	NA
Other district activities (voluntary participation)	63	65	NA
Enrollment in graduate courses at an institution of higher education	63	36	38
State department of education or county agency activity (voluntary participation)	50	51	NA
State department of education or county agency activity (required participation)	30	25	NA
Principal Center or Academy (voluntary participation)	25	26	NA
National meeting of NASSP	NA	NA	30
National meeting of other educational organizations	NA	NA	27
State meetings of principals' associations	NA	NA	76
State meetings of other educational organizations	NA	NA	55
Travel for visitation outside the district	NA	NA	54
Involvement in a formal project or research in education	NA	NA	22
Participation in conferences and workshops, not included above and outside the district	NA	NA	62
Participation in conferences and workshops within district	NA	NA	79
Participation in a study group on a planned, regular basis not included above	NA	NA	29

36 percent for all respondents, but 63 percent for first-year principals.

- Attendance at state meetings of principal associations in 1977 (76 percent) is comparable to the 73 percent reporting voluntary participation in 1987.

- In 1987, respondents report required participation (69 percent) and voluntary participation (65 percent) in professional activities within the employing school district. Comparable data are not available for 1977.

- During the 1980s, state departments or county agencies, partially in response to the many reports that addressed issues of educational reform, increased the number and range of professional activities available to principals. Voluntary participation in such activities was reported by 51 percent of the respondents in the 1987 study.

- Although no comparable data exist for 1977, respondents to the 1987 survey reported a relatively high level (45 percent) of voluntary participation in activities conducted by private consultants at out-of-district workshops.

The data in Table 5.14 support the conclusion that principals are involved in many kinds of professional development activities and that for the most part, participation is voluntary. The typical principal reported participation in four or five different types of activities during the two years preceding the 1987 survey.

Summary

Most principals have baccalaureate majors in social sciences, physical education, humanities, or education. The level of formal education completed by principals has steadily increased since 1965; in 1987, the master's degree was the minimal academic qualification and 13 percent of the principals possessed an earned doctoral degree.

Teaching and administrative experience are common preparation for persons selected as principals. Most principals in 1987 had seven to nine years in the classroom before appointment. More than half of all practicing principals have prior experience as coaches and many have served as department chairpersons, athletic directors, or guidance counselors.

The average age at which individuals are selected for the principalship increased between 1965 and 1977 and again between 1977 and 1987. A number of factors influence appointment to the principalship, especially quality and quantity of professional preparation, a successful job interview, being "wanted" by the superintendent, and success as an assistant principal. Persons enter the principalship with more experience, training, and later in life than was formerly true.

The school environment (student discipline, parental support) tops the list of factors that influence career movement within education. Generally, younger principals work in smaller schools and older principals in larger schools. The typical career path proceeds from smaller schools in less urban settings to larger schools in suburban or urban locations. An upward trend can be documented over the past two decades in principals' satisfaction with their choice of career. Most principals plan to remain in the principalship; those interested in moving generally aspire to the superintendency or other central office position. Little movement takes place from the elementary principalship to the secondary principalship, or vice-versa.

Principals participate in a wide variety of professional activities at the local, state, and national levels.

# VI Profiles of Leaders and Schools

The senior high school is a complex organization in an increasingly complex society. Over the years, principals have accepted more and more managerial and supervisory responsibilities. How principals respond to the various expectations others have for them and the personal dilemmas that come from the role expectations they hold for themselves are questions that motivated this study.

American schools have been inundated in this decade with a series of national reports that have chronicled the ill health of public education while calling for sweeping reform for the benefit of society. The widespread educational reform movement, coupled with a rapid movement from an industrial to an informational society, causes Americans to rethink the goals, programs, and operating structures of their secondary schools. What will be the ultimate effect of these movements on senior high schools and those who have the responsibility to lead them?

A series of research questions posed in the introduction to this report raised issues about American schools and their leaders in the 1980s. This chapter summarizes the answers to those questions as organized and reported in the preceding chapters of this volume.

1. The personal/professional characteristics and opinions of senior high school principals and assistant principals.

2. Their job-related tasks and problems.

3. The characteristics of senior high school programs and teachers.

4. The role assistant principals play in the school leadership team.

5. The career patterns in the principalship.

The profiles in the remainder of this chapter provide a summary of the study and culminate in a few of the more notable findings and conclusions.

CHARACTERISTICS AND OPINIONS

Personal and Professional Characteristics

1. The typical high school principal is a white male between 40 and 55 years of age. Female principals are more likely to be found on the West Coast, in cities with populations of 150,000 or more, and in schools other than public comprehensive. Non-white principals are

more prevalent on the West Coast, in the Southwest, and in cities with populations of 150,000 or more.

2. The typical high school assistant principal is a white male between 35 and 50 years of age. Women now comprise 18 percent of the assistant principals in American schools and are more likely to be found on the West Coast, in the South, and in New England, and less likely in smaller cities, towns, and rural areas. Non-white assistant principals are more numerous in the South and Southwest, and in cities with populations greater than 150,000.

Salaries, Benefits, and Tenure

3. After a fairly rapid increase from 1965 to 1977, school administrator salaries appear to have reached a plateau in the past 10 years. The differential between principal and teacher salaries has narrowed. Older principals and assistant principals receive higher salaries, but for assistant principals, age beyond 40 is not related to salary.

4. Non-white principals receive higher salaries than white principals, but this finding is confounded by region of the country in which these principals live and the size of the schools in which they work. The relationship between ethnicity and salary does not hold for assistant principals.

5. Principals and assistant principals in the Mid-Atlantic and West Coast regions tend to receive somewhat higher salaries. These higher salaries are likely a result of the higher cost of living in these two regions. Principals in larger schools also tend to receive higher salaries, presumably because of their seniority and greater responsibilities.

6. On the average, male and female principals receive similar salaries. The distribution of female salaries tends to be somewhat bi-modal, with principals of parochial and private schools receiving lower salaries and principals of public alternative and public specialized schools receiving higher salaries.

7. Most principals and assistant principals receive medical, retirement, life insurance, and dental benefits.

8. Few principals or assistant principals hold administrative tenure, but the vast majority believe that they should. Most have annual contracts of 11 or 12 months (principals) or 10 to 12 months (assistant principals).

Opinions About Certification and Educational Issues

9. The vast majority of principals and assistant principals believe that specific administrative courses, a teaching certificate, teaching experience, a master's degree, specific curriculum and instruction

courses, and an internship should be required for principal certification. Certification requirements proposed more recently, such as assessment center participation, written professional examination, and on-the-job monitoring, are reported by fewer than 40 percent of principals and assistant principals.

10. The opinions expressed by current principals make it clear that the principalship is changing. Many of the educational issues endorsed by a large percentage of current principals were not even included in previous surveys. Unfortunately, the broad pattern of this change is not clear. Some of the opinions of current principals more closely resemble those of the principals in the 1965 survey; others resemble those of principals in the 1977 survey. A few issues have garnered increasing support during the past two decades. Topping the current poll are the principle of universal education in American society, school programs for alcohol and drug abuse, programs for the academically talented, and teacher evaluation based on teaching effectiveness criteria.

TASKS AND PROBLEMS

Roles and Responsibilities

1. Principals are more concerned with new educational directions than day-to-day operations, personal initiative than outside influences, and collaborative rather than unilateral decision making.

2. Principals in larger schools have bigger administrative teams to help them with administrative tasks and problems. However, principals in very large schools and those in very small schools are least satisfied with the quality of their administrative support. Perhaps principals in the largest schools feel that they never have enough support, while principals in the smallest schools actually receive very little.

3. The principalship is a very time-consuming job. The majority of principals work more than 55 hours per week. The percentage of principals who work fewer than 50 hours per week has declined during the past two decades. Assistant principals also work long hours, spending on the average 50 hours or more per week on the job.

4. Principals spend relatively more time on school management than on any other administrative task. Principals believe, however, that program development should be their first priority. The discrepancies between the ways principals actually spend their time and what they believe they should do have not changed during the past decade.

67

5. Few principals have teaching responsibilities, but the majority spend more than four hours per week conducting informal observations in classrooms. Over the years, actual teaching by principals has given way to the supervision of teaching.

6. An erosion of principal authority is evident during the past decade, particularly in staffing practices and staff selection. Despite this erosion, however, principals report having more opportunity for independent thought and action than in the past and are quite satisfied with their jobs.

Roadblocks and Influences

7. Several problems or conditions interfere with principals and assistant principals on the job. The most frequently cited roadblocks are the amount of time spent on administrative detail, a general lack of time to do the job, an inability to secure necessary funds, apathetic or irresponsible parents, new state guidelines and requirements, and a lack of time to administer and supervise student activities. Several problems cited in previous surveys appear less troublesome today, including variations in the ability of teachers, insufficient space and physical facilities, and problem students. In combination, the drop in importance of these conditions suggests improved working conditions for principals during the past 20 years.

8. Collective bargaining exists in approximately three of five school districts. Fortunately, the presence of collective bargaining has had little impact on principals' or assistant principals' working relationships with central office administration or teachers.

9. A large number of external factors are likely to affect principals and their schools during the next three to five years. Chief among these influences are the personalized/effective education movement, child abuse, community participation, community-based learning, and teen sexual activity. A sizable minority of principals also believe that youth gang activity, youth unemployment, and changes in enrollment will have a strong influence on their schools.

10. Athletic, band, and music boosters and teachers' organizations are the special interest groups that exert the greatest influence on principals. Contrary to popular opinion, censorship groups and extremist individuals or groups have little influence. In fact, the influence of these special interest groups has declined during the past two decades. The majority of principals believe that parent and community participation should be limited to fund raising, general volunteer services, development of school disciplinary rules, and supervision of student activities. Few principals support

parental involvement in matters of curriculum and instruction, and virtually none believe that parents or community members should be involved in personnel decisions.

Job Characteristics and Satisfaction

11. Principals and assistant principals rate their jobs highly in terms of opportunity to help others, job security, prestige, independent thought and action, and self-fulfillment. The ratings on these job characteristics have improved during the past 20 years. Assistant principals differ from principals primarily in associating lower prestige and lower levels of self-fulfillment with their jobs. Indeed, the vast majority of principals and assistant principals are either satisfied or very satisfied with most aspects of their jobs (i.e., interpersonal relations, realization of expectations, results, and working conditions). Both principals and assistant principals are least satisfied with their salaries and the time they must spend on the job.

SCHOOL PROGRAM AND STAFFING

Student-Related Factors

1. Expenditures per student roughly doubled between 1977 and 1987. About 7 percent of the high schools in the 1987 sample spent less than $1,500 per student. At the upper end of the expenditure scale, 7 percent spent more than $5,000 per student. There were no low expenditure schools in New England or the noncontiguous states (Alaska and Hawaii); 43 percent of the schools in this category were from the South.

2. Important gains were made between 1977 and 1987 in average daily attendance (ADA), retention rate, and percent of students entering college. In 1987, 33 percent of the schools in the sample had an ADA of 95 percent or better, versus 17 percent of the schools in 1977. In 1965, 62 percent of the schools reported a dropout rate of less than 10 percent. By 1977, this level of retention was achieved by 67 percent of the schools, and by 1987, by 80 percent. Schools reporting more than 40 percent of their students going on to college constituted 37 percent of the sample in 1965, 62 percent in 1977, and 75 percent in 1987.

Teaching Staff

3. Principals believe that the most important teacher skills are competence in subject matter, competence in adjusting instruction to varying student needs, interpersonal skills in working with students, competence in methods of instruction, and skill in developing positive student self-concept.

4. Forty-nine percent of the principals reported that up to one-fourth of their teachers had one preparation per day. Thirty-eight percent said that up to 25 percent of their teachers had four or more preparations per day. Homeroom exists in only 60 percent of the schools and is used mainly for attendance and administrative functions.

5. The male-to-female ratio of teachers has continued to decline during the past two decades. In 1987, 49 percent of the schools reported that the percentage of males was less than half of the teaching faculty, while in both 1977 and 1965, only 36 percent of the schools reported this ratio.

Curriculum and Program

6. Teachers are the most important influence in subject content and textbook and library book selection by an overwhelming margin over administrators, district supervisors, board members, and parents.

7. Graduation requirements have increased in mathematics, science, computer skills, and English/language arts.

8. Ability grouping is practiced in about half the high schools reporting. Seventy-three percent of the schools in the sample reported some form of special provisions for the gifted and talented.

9. Advanced technology is widely used in schools for administrative purposes as well as for library and media operations and for teacher test construction and scoring.

10. Principal ranking of educational purposes revealed minor changes between 1977 and 1987; significant changes occurred between 1965 and 1977. Acquisition of basic skills, positive self-concept, and skills in critical inquiry and problem solving retained rankings of first, second, and third. Preparation for a changing world moved from eighth to fourth place while preparation for family life moved from sixth to ninth place.

11. Forty-eight percent of the principals favor checks on basic skills attainment; an additional 20 percent have a working system. Thirty-nine percent favor individualized promotion; an additional 6 percent have a system to accomplish it.

12. More than half the principals reported the impact of the current reform movement as strong or moderate in creating new initiatives in instruction, staffing, and student services and involvement.

THE ASSISTANT PRINCIPALSHIP

Duties and Responsibilities

1. More similarities than differences emerge when the role of the assistant principal in 1987 is compared with the role in 1965.

2. Variety is an important aspect of the assistant principal's job. Assistant principals have responsibility for a wide range of duties scattered across all six of the major task categories examined in the study. There is not a single duty among the 65 listed for review for which some assistant principal does not have some measure of responsibility.

3. Some shifts in the duties of assistant principals occurred between the 1965 and 1987 studies. Many traditional functions in school management and student services still remain at the heart of the assistant principalship, but several new priorities have emerged. Assistant principals by 1987 had assumed greater responsibility for teacher evaluation and teacher selection. An increasing emphasis on these duties may signal the beginnings of an enhanced role for the assistant principal as an instructional leader.

4. The assistant principalship is viewed both by principals and assistant principals as a very responsible position, but principals generally perceive assistant principals as having less responsibility for delegated duties than assistant principals see themselves. Assistant principals are not generally given full responsibility for delegated behaviors; principals tend to maintain some degree of personal responsibility for all the administrative tasks of the school. Shared rather than full responsibility seems to be the favored form of delegation. In fact, the assistant principalship could be described as a "sharing role."

5. Assistant principals perform many important duties in the high school. A close correlation exists between the level of responsibility assistant principals have for performing various duties, and the perception of both principals and assistant principals that these duties are important to the proper functioning of the school.

6. Assistant principals exercise considerable discretion in carrying out their major delegated responsibilities. Principals do tend to delegate authority with responsibility, as evidenced by the close relationship reported in the current study between the degree of responsibility assistant principals have for a duty and their level of discretion for carrying it out. Nevertheless, assistant principals in 1987 report less overall discretion in carrying out their duties than their counterparts did in 1965.

7. The views of principals and assistant principals about duties and responsibilities diverged more in 1987 than in 1965. Contributing to this divergence, perhaps, is the rather startling finding that almost one-half of assistant principals are not consulted about the assignment of their job responsibilities. This finding likely reflects tradition and the current environment of accountability in education

71

rather than any developing rift among building-level administrators.

8. The assistant principal is a vital part of the school administrative team. Given the broad range of responsibilities delegated to them, the importance of these responsibilities, and the skill and judgment required to carry them out, it is difficult to imagine how most high schools could operate effectively without the day-to-day contributions of their assistant principals. As schools attempt to respond to a more diverse student population and to meet the learning needs of more students, the assistant principal may well assume an increasingly important role in the functioning principalship.

CAREER PATTERNS OF PRINCIPALS

Preparation

1. Most principals have baccalaureate majors in one of five areas: social sciences (24 percent); sciences (20 percent); physical education (16 percent); humanities (14 percent); or education (14 percent). Diversity at the baccalaureate level has been a relatively constant factor in the findings for 1965, 1977, and 1987.

2. The level of formal education completed by principals has steadily increased since 1965. In 1965, 10 percent of the principals surveyed did not have a master's degree and only 1 percent had a doctoral degree. By 1987, the master's degree was reported as the minimal academic qualification, and 13 percent of the principals possessed an earned doctorate. Indeed, 38 percent of the 1987 sample held a specialist degree or higher.

3. Substantial teaching experience is common to persons selected as principals. Comparative data are not available from the 1965 or 1977 studies, but most principals in 1987 had 7 to 9 years in the classroom before appointment. Almost half of all persons entering the principalship in 1987 had 10 or more years of teaching experience.

4. Some form of administrative or quasi-administrative experience is typical before selection to the principalship. Only 20 percent of the 1987 sample moved into the position directly from the role of classroom teacher. More than half of all practicing principals have prior experience as coaches (52 percent). Other common professional experiences before selection include service as department chairperson (46 percent), athletic director (28 percent), or guidance counselor (28 percent).

Appointment and Longevity

5. The average age at which individuals are selected for the role of principal increased between 1965 and 1977 and again between 1977 and 1987.

72

6. A number of factors influence appointment to the principalship. In order of perceived importance, these are: quality and quantity of professional preparation, a successful job interview, being "wanted" by the superintendent, success as an assistant principal, contacts within the profession, success as a teacher, and "luck." An emerging trend is the use of assessment center reports in selection decisions.

7. Persons enter the principalship with more experience, training, and at older ages than was true in the past. They tend to remain in the role, are in the same position for an average of five years or more, and are satisfied with their choice of career. Almost half of all principals who responded in 1987 had been in the same position for six or more years; in 1965, only 40 percent had served that long in the same position.

Career Patterns and Satisfaction

8. A number of factors influence career movement: family commitments, the location of a school or school district, the school environment (student discipline, parental support), and issues related to job security. Each of these factors is perceived by principals as important.

9. In 1965, 1977, and 1987, younger principals worked in schools with smaller student populations, and older principals, in schools with larger student populations. The career ladder for most principals is a progression from smaller schools in less urban settings to larger schools in suburban or urban locations.

10. Since 1965, an upward trend can be documented in the levels of satisfaction reported by principals about their choice of career. Seventy-one percent of the principals surveyed in 1987 reported satisfaction with the principalship; only 14 percent reported any dissatisfaction.

11. Most principals plan to remain in the principalship. Those who plan to move generally aspire to a position in central office administration, including the superintendency. Data from the 1987 study support the conclusion that there is little movement, or desire to move, from the elementary principalship to the secondary principalship, or vice-versa.

12. Principals are engaged in a wide variety of professional activities at the local, state, and national levels. State association activities (73 percent), school district activities (65 to 69 percent), and national association meetings (54 percent) showed the greatest percentage of participation.

SIGNIFICANT FINDINGS

The majority of the findings in this study are within the realm of predictability. Most reflect normal evolution in the functions and tasks of American education and school administration. but a few stand out.

1. The typical principal or assistant principal is a white male between 35 and 55 years of age. Female principals are more likely to be found on the West Coast, in cities of 150,000 or more, and in schools other than public comprehensive. Almost one in five assistant principals is now female, suggesting the potential for more women in the high school principalship in the near future. Female assistant principals are more numerous in the West, South, and New England, and less so in smaller cities, towns, and rural areas. Non-white principals are more prevalent in the West and South, and in cities of 150,000 or more. Non-white assistant principals are found more in the South and Southwest, and in cities of 150,000 or more.

2. School administrator salaries have virtually leveled off since 1977. The salary differential between teachers and principals has narrowed to the point that the average teacher salary minus the average principal salary is less than it was 10 years ago.

3. Many of the educational issues endorsed as important by a large percentage of principals in the 1987 survey were not even included in earlier surveys. Notable among this group are programs for alcohol and drug abuse, teacher evaluation based on teaching effectiveness criteria, functional computer competence for students, and more stringent requirements in the traditional academic subjects.

4. An overwhelming majority of principals are more concerned with new educational directions than the day-to-day management of the schools, policy development and implementation based on personal initiative and judgment rather than merely representing the interests of parents or patrons, and shared decision making with the faculty rather than unilateral action on important issues.

5. Erosion is evident in principals' authority during the past decade, particularly in staff selection and staffing practices. In 1977, 92 percent of those surveyed reported unrestricted or only moderately restricted authority in staff selection; the comparable figure for 1987 was 67 percent.

6. Principals continue to rank time or lack of time for administrative detail as their chief roadblock, but several problems emphasized in earlier surveys are less troublesome today, particularly variations in teacher ability, problem students, and insufficient space and physical facilities. In this sense, working conditions for principals seem to have improved during the past 20 years.

7. Principals believe that the personalized/effective education movement and the issue of child abuse will have the greatest influence on their own schools during the next three to five years.

8. The majority of principals believe that parent and community participation in the school should be limited to fund raising, general

volunteer services, development of school discipline rules, and supervision of student activities. One-third or less support involvement in matters of curriculum and instruction.

9. Important gains have been made between 1977 and 1987 in average daily attendance, retention rate, and percentage of students entering college. Schools reporting a 95 percent ADA or better increased from 17 percent in 1977 to 33 percent in 1987. Schools reporting a retention rate of 90 percent or better rose from 62 percent in 1965, to 67 percent in 1977, to 80 percent in 1987. Schools reporting college attendance rates of 40 percent or more increased from 37 percent in 1965, to 62 percent in 1977, to 75 percent in 1987.

10. The male-to-female ratio in teaching staff has declined since the last study. Thirty-six percent of the schools in 1977 reported that males were less than half the faculty. Forty-nine percent reported that ratio in 1987.

11. Assistant principals have assumed greater responsibility for teacher evaluation and teacher selection during the past decade. Conversely, some traditional duties in school management and student activities are reported less frequently.

12. Principals generally perceive assistant principals as having less responsibility for delegated duties than assistant principals themselves believe. Assistant principals usually are given shared rather than full responsibility for a delegated task. Assistant principals exercise considerable discretion in carrying out these responsibilities, but they report less overall discretion in 1987 than their counterparts did in 1965. Greater divergence exists in 1987 between the views of principals and assistant principals about the latter's duties than was reported in 1965.

13. The assistant principal in most high schools is delegated a broad range of duties that carry with them considerable responsibility, importance, and discretionary behavior. The role of the assistant principal is vital to the functioning administrative team at the school building level.

14. Educators enter the principalship today with more experience, training, and at older ages than in the past. On the average, they tend to stay in the principalship for nine or more years, and to remain in the same school for six years or longer.

15. In general, the principals of the late 1980s, when compared to principals in earlier surveys, are more satisfied with their career choice, more committed to their profession, and more active in professional development. Principals today identify strongly with the principalship as a present and future career role.

Appendix A: The Survey Instruments

NATIONAL ASSOCIATION OF SECONDARY SCHOOL PRINCIPALS

Reston, Virginia 22091

A National Study of High School Leaders and Their Schools

SURVEY OF HIGH SCHOOL PRINCIPALS

Form A

DIRECTIONS

Your questionnaire is identified by the label placed on it. It is not necessary to sign or place your name on the questionnaire. In reporting results, only statistical summaries of the responses of groups of principals will be cited. In no case will the identity of an individual be divulged. You are urged to make every answer a sincere one.

Circle the number of the appropriate response using pen or pencil. If you change a response, please make the change distinctly so there is no doubt about how you wish to answer.

Attempt to answer every question. For some questions none of the alternatives may correspond exactly to your situation or to the opinion you hold. In such cases mark the alternative which comes closest to the answer you would like to give.

Place your completed questionnaire in the envelope provided and mail it to NASSP. Thank you for your cooperation and assistance in this important study.

••

Advisory Committee for A Study of High School Leaders and Their Schools:

Patricia D. Campbell, Lakewood High School, Lakewood, Colorado; Glen M. DeHaven, Oldtown School, Oldtown, Maryland; Richard Gorton, School of Education, University of Wisconsin–Milwaukee; Jacqueline H. Simmons, Paul Robeson High School, Chicago, Illinois; Norman O. Stevens, Mill River Union High School, North Clarendon, Vermont; Michael K. Thomas, Vashon High School, St. Louis, Missouri; Peggy Walters, J. Frank Dobie High School, Houston, Texas; Gary P. Wells, Henley High School, Klamath Falls, Oregon; Jeannette Wheatley, Cass Technical High School, Detroit, Michigan; James V. Wright, Fremont Ross High School, Fremont, Ohio.

Research Team:

Lorin W. Anderson, University of South Carolina; Edgar A. Kelley, Western Michigan University; Lloyd E. McCleary, University of Utah; Leonard O. Pellicer, University of South Carolina; James W. Keefe, NASSP

1. What is your sex?   (01) Male   (02) Female

2. What is your age?

   (01) 23 or under   (04) 35-39   (07) 50-54
   (02) 24-29   (05) 40-44   (08) 55-59
   (03) 30-34   (06) 45-49   (09) 60 or older

3. With which ethnic group would you identify yourself?

   (01) White   (03) Hispanic   (05) Asian
   (02) Black   (04) American Indian   (06) Other: _____

4. In which of the following areas did you major as an **undergraduate? *Select only one answer.***

   (01) Secondary education (other than physical education)
   (02) Physical education
   (03) Elementary education
   (04) Humanities (literature, languages, etc.)
   (05) Physical or biological sciences
   (06) Social sciences (sociology, history, etc.)
   (07) Mathematics
   (08) Fine arts
   (09) Business
   (10) Vocational-Technical (home economics, industrial arts, etc.)
   (11) Other: _____

5. What is the highest degree you have earned?

   (01) Less than a BA
   (02) Bachelor's Degree
   (03) Master's Degree in Education
   (04) Master's Degree not in Education
   (05) Master's Degree plus some additional graduate work
   (06) Educational Specialist, six-year program or equivalent
   (07) Master's Degree plus *all course work* for a doctorate
   (08) Doctor of Education
   (09) Doctor of Philosophy
   (10) Other: _____

6. How many years of ***teaching*** experience, regardless of level, did you have prior to taking your present position? Do not include years as a full-time administrator, supervisor, counselor, psychologist, or librarian.

   (01) None   (04) 4-6 years   (07) 15-19 years
   (02) One year   (05) 7-9 years   (08) 20-24 years
   (03) 2-3 years   (06) 10-14 years   (09) 25 or more years

7. What was the last position you held prior to becoming a high school principal? ***Select only one answer.***

   (01) Teacher
   (02) Assistant principal of an elementary or middle level school
   (03) Assistant principal of a high school
   (04) Principal of an elementary or middle level school
   (05) Guidance counselor
   (06) Other—education, specify: _____
   (07) Other—non-education, specify: _____

8. At what age were you appointed to your first principalship?

   (01) 23 or under   (04) 35-39   (07) 50-54
   (02) 24-29   (05) 40-44   (08) 55-59
   (03) 30-34   (06) 45-49   (09) 60 or older

9. How many years have you served as a principal, including this school year?

(01) One year   (04) 6-7 years   (07) 15-19 years
(02) 2-3 years   (05) 8-9 years   (08) 20-24 years
(03) 4-5 years   (06) 10-14 years   (09) 25 or more years

10. How long have you been a principal in this school, including this school year?

(01) One year   (04) 4-5 years   (07) 12-14 years
(02) Two years   (05) 6-8 years   (08) 15-17 years
(03) Three years   (06) 9-11 years   (09) 18 or more years

11. Which of the following categories best describes the school of which you are principal? *Choose only one answer.*

(01) Public comprehensive   (05) Private, religious affiliated
(02) Public "alternative"   (06) Private, not religious affiliated
(03) Public special (commercial, vocational, arts, etc.)   (07) Other, specify _____
(04) Parochial or diocesan

12. What grades are included in your school?

(01) Kindergarten-12   (05) 9-12
(02) 1-12   (06) 10-12
(03) 7-12   (07) 11-12
(04) 8-12   (08) Other, specify _____

13. How many high school students (grade 9 and above) were enrolled in your school on October 1st of the current school year?

(01) Fewer than 250   (04) 750-999   (07) 2,000-2,499
(02) 250-499   (05) 1,000-1,499   (08) 2,500 or more
(03) 500-749   (06) 1,500-1,999

14. In which geographic region is your school located?

(01) New England   (04) Midwest   (07) West Coast
(02) Mid-Atlantic   (05) Southwest   (08) Non-contiguous
(03) South   (06) Inter Mountain   (09) Other, specify _____

15. What is the average per-student expenditure for each high school student in your school for the current school year (exclusive of capital outlay)?

(01) Less than $1,500   (04) 2,500-2,999   (07) 4,000-4,499
(02) 1,500-1,999   (05) 3,000-3,499   (08) 4,500-4,999
(03) 2,000-2,499   (06) 3,500-3,999   (09) 5,000 or more

16. Which of the following population categories best describes the locale of the high school in which you are principal?

(01) City, more than 1,000,000   (04) City, 25,000-149,999, distinct from a metropolitan area
(02) City, 150,000-999,999   (05) City, 5,000-24,999, not suburban
(03) Suburban, related to city of 150,000 or more   (06) Town or rural under 5,000

17. What would you estimate is the percent of average daily attendance of those enrolled in your school for the current school year?

(01) Less than 50%   (03) 71% to 80%   (05) 91% to 95%
(02) 50% to 70%   (04) 81% to 90%   (06) 96% or more

18. What percentage of all pupils who enter the first year at your school drop out before graduation? Do not include those who transfer to another school.

(01) Less than 5%   (04) 20% to 29%   (07) 60% to 79%
(02) 5% to 9%   (05) 30% to 39%   (08) 80% to 99%
(03) 10% to 19%   (06) 40% to 59%

19. What percentage of the students in your current graduating class are college bound?

(01) Less than 5%   (04) 20% to 29%   (07) 60% to 79%
(02) 5% to 9%   (05) 30% to 39%   (08) 80% to 94%
(03) 10% to 19%   (06) 40% to 59%   (09) 95% or more

20. What is your current annual salary as principal? Do not include fringe benefits.

(01) Less than $25,000   (04) 35,000-39,999   (07) 50,000-54,999
(02) 25,000-29,999   (05) 40,000-44,999   (08) 55,000-59,999
(03) 30,000-34,999   (06) 45,000-49,999   (09) 60,000 or more
                                                    (10) Not applicable (religious order)

21. On the average, how many hours a week do you work at your job as principal?

(01) Less than 40   (03) 45-49   (05) 55-59
(02) 40-44   (04) 50-54   (06) 60 or more

22. How do you spend your time during the typical work week? Rank these nine areas according to the amount of time spent in each area.

In Column A, mark a "1" next to the area in which you *do spend* the most time, ranking all areas until you have marked a "9" next to the area in which you spend the least time.

Then, in Column B, mark a "1" next to the area in which you feel you *should spend* the most time, ranking all items accordingly until you have marked a "9" next to the area in which you feel you should spend the least time.

A. DO Spend Time	Area of Responsibility	SHOULD Spend Time
_____	(01) *Program Development* (curriculum, instructional leadership, etc.)	_____
_____	(02) *Personnel* (evaluating, advising, conferring, recruiting, etc.)	_____
_____	(03) *Management* (weekly calendar, office, budget, memos, etc.)	_____
_____	(04) *Student Activities* (meetings, supervision, planning, etc.)	_____
_____	(05) *Student Behavior* (discipline, attendance, meetings, etc.)	_____
_____	(06) *Community* (PTA, advisory groups, parent conferences, etc.)	_____
_____	(07) *District Office* (meetings, task forces, reports, etc.)	_____
_____	(08) *Professional Development* (reading, conferences, etc.)	_____
_____	(09) *Planning* (annual, long range)	_____

23. *Duties and Responsibilities of Assistant Principals.* Principals have final responsibility for everything that happens in a school, but assistant principals share in differing degrees in that responsibility. Please indicate the job profile of the assistant principal(s) in your school in the following chart. Please check the "not applicable" box for any function that does not apply.

Directions:

RESPONSIBILITY	IMPORTANCE	DISCRETIONARY BEHAVIOR
In the appropriate column, indicate the **degree of responsibility** assistant principals have for each duty delegated. Circle the number: (01) Slight —The principal does the job. APs may aid at his direction. (02) Shared—Delegated with close supervision; principal and assistant principals work together. (03) Full —Delegated with general supervision; assistant principals are held responsible for the job.	In the appropriate column, indicate the **degree of importance** you believe the **delegated** duty has to the proper functioning of the school. Circle the number: (01) Least importance (02) Minor importance (03) Average importance (04) Major importance (05) Most importance	In the appropriate column, indicate your judgment of the **level of discretionary** behavior involved in the completion of any **delegated** duty in **your** school. (A duty may be of relatively minor importance and yet it could involve high discretionary behavior. The reverse may be equally true.) Circle the number: (01) Low —Behavior that is directed in large measure by others; behavior that involves restricted high order decision making. (02) High —Behavior that is self-directing, involving high order decision making.

	SAMPLE RESPONSES										
	NOT APPLICABLE	Degree of Responsibility			Degree of Importance					Level of Discretionary Behavior	
Illustrated Examples Responsibility for:		SLIGHT	SHARED	FULL	LEAST	MINOR	AVERAGE	MAJOR	MOST	LOW	HIGH
01 Faculty Socials	☐	1	2	③	1	②	3	4	5	1	②
02 "Career day" conferences	☐	①	2	3	1	2	3	④	5	①	2
03 Report card procedures	☑	1	2	3	1	2	3	4	5	1	2

	NOT APPLICABLE	Degree of Responsibility			Degree of Importance					Level of Discretionary Behavior	
Circle Appropriate Code Numbers (For an item that is not applicable to your school situation, place a check (✔) in the NA box after the item).		SLIGHT	SHARED	FULL	LEAST	MINOR	AVERAGE	MAJOR	MOST	LOW	HIGH
Responsibility for:											
Curriculum and Instruction											
(01) Articulation with feeder schools	☐	1	2	3	1	2	3	4	5	1	2
(02) Curriculum development	☐	1	2	3	1	2	3	4	5	1	2
(03) Evaluation of teachers	☐	1	2	3	1	2	3	4	5	1	2
(04) Innovations, experiments, and research	☐	1	2	3	1	2	3	4	5	1	2
(05) Instructional media and materials	☐	1	2	3	1	2	3	4	5	1	2
(06) Instructional methods	☐	1	2	3	1	2	3	4	5	1	2
(07) Instructional software	☐	1	2	3	1	2	3	4	5	1	2
(08) School-wide examinations	☐	1	2	3	1	2	3	4	5	1	2
(09) School master schedule	☐	1	2	3	1	2	3	4	5	1	2
(10) Staff inservice	☐	1	2	3	1	2	3	4	5	1	2
(11) Textbook selection	☐	1	2	3	1	2	3	4	5	1	2
(12) Work-study program	☐	1	2	3	1	2	3	4	5	1	2
Responsibility for:											
Community Relations											
(13) Administrative representative at community functions	☐	1	2	3	1	2	3	4	5	1	2
(14) Adult education program	☐	1	2	3	1	2	3	4	5	1	2
(15) Coordinating community resources for instruction	☐	1	2	3	1	2	3	4	5	1	2
(16) Informing public of school achievements	☐	1	2	3	1	2	3	4	5	1	2
(17) Liaison with community youth-serving agencies	☐	1	2	3	1	2	3	4	5	1	2
(18) Parent-Teacher Association	☐	1	2	3	1	2	3	4	5	1	2
(19) School alumni association	☐	1	2	3	1	2	3	4	5	1	2
(20) School public relations program	☐	1	2	3	1	2	3	4	5	1	2
(21) School participation in community fund drives	☐	1	2	3	1	2	3	4	5	1	2
Responsibility for:											
School Management											
(22) Building use—nonschool-related	☐	1	2	3	1	2	3	4	5	1	2
(23) Building use—school-related	☐	1	2	3	1	2	3	4	5	1	2
(24) Cafeteria services	☐	1	2	3	1	2	3	4	5	1	2
(25) Clerical services	☐	1	2	3	1	2	3	4	5	1	2
(26) Computer services	☐	1	2	3	1	2	3	4	5	1	2
(27) Custodial services	☐	1	2	3	1	2	3	4	5	1	2

Circle Appropriate Code Numbers (For an item that is not applicable to your school situation, place a check (✔) in the NA box after the item).	NOT APPLICABLE	Degree of Responsibility			Degree of Importance					Level of Discretionary Behavior	
		SLIGHT	SHARED	FULL	LEAST	MINOR	AVERAGE	MAJOR	MOST	LOW	HIGH
(28) Emergency arrangements	☐	1	2	3	1	2	3	4	5	1	2
(29) Graduation activities	☐	1	2	3	1	2	3	4	5	1	2
(30) Noninstructional equipment and supplies	☐	1	2	3	1	2	3	4	5	1	2
(31) School budget	☐	1	2	3	1	2	3	4	5	1	2
(32) School calendars	☐	1	2	3	1	2	3	4	5	1	2
(33) School daily bulletins	☐	1	2	3	1	2	3	4	5	1	2
(34) School financial accounts	☐	1	2	3	1	2	3	4	5	1	2
(35) School policies	☐	1	2	3	1	2	3	4	5	1	2
(36) Special arrangements at start and close of school year	☐	1	2	3	1	2	3	4	5	1	2
(37) Transportation services	☐	1	2	3	1	2	3	4	5	1	2

Responsibility for:

Staff Personnel

	NOT APPLICABLE	SLIGHT	SHARED	FULL	LEAST	MINOR	AVERAGE	MAJOR	MOST	LOW	HIGH
(38) Faculty meetings	☐	1	2	3	1	2	3	4	5	1	2
(39) Orientation program for new teachers	☐	1	2	3	1	2	3	4	5	1	2
(40) Student teachers	☐	1	2	3	1	2	3	4	5	1	2
(41) Substitute teachers	☐	1	2	3	1	2	3	4	5	1	2
(42) Teacher "duty" rosters	☐	1	2	3	1	2	3	4	5	1	2
(43) Teacher personnel records	☐	1	2	3	1	2	3	4	5	1	2
(44) Teacher incentives, motivation	☐	1	2	3	1	2	3	4	5	1	2
(45) Teacher selection	☐	1	2	3	1	2	3	4	5	1	2

Responsibility for:

Student Activities

	NOT APPLICABLE	SLIGHT	SHARED	FULL	LEAST	MINOR	AVERAGE	MAJOR	MOST	LOW	HIGH
(46) Assemblies	☐	1	2	3	1	2	3	4	5	1	2
(47) Athletic program	☐	1	2	3	1	2	3	4	5	1	2
(48) School club program	☐	1	2	3	1	2	3	4	5	1	2
(49) School dances	☐	1	2	3	1	2	3	4	5	1	2
(50) School newspaper	☐	1	2	3	1	2	3	4	5	1	2
(51) School traffic or safety squad	☐	1	2	3	1	2	3	4	5	1	2
(52) Student council	☐	1	2	3	1	2	3	4	5	1	2
(53) Student photographs	☐	1	2	3	1	2	3	4	5	1	2
(54) Student store	☐	1	2	3	1	2	3	4	5	1	2

Responsibility for:

Student Services

	NOT APPLICABLE	SLIGHT	SHARED	FULL	LEAST	MINOR	AVERAGE	MAJOR	MOST	LOW	HIGH
(55) Financial aid for students	☐	1	2	3	1	2	3	4	5	1	2
(56) Guidance program	☐	1	2	3	1	2	3	4	5	1	2
(57) Instruction for home-bound students	☐	1	2	3	1	2	3	4	5	1	2

Circle Appropriate Code Numbers (For an item that is not applicable to your school situation, place a check (✔) in the NA box after the item).	NOT APPLICABLE	Degree of Responsibility			Degree of Importance					Level of Discretionary Behavior	
		SLIGHT	SHARED	FULL	LEAST	MINOR	AVERAGE	MAJOR	MOST	LOW	HIGH
(58) Medical, dental, and health services	☐	1	2	3	1	2	3	4	5	1	2
(59) Orientation program for new students	☐	1	2	3	1	2	3	4	5	1	2
(60) Relationships with educational and employer representatives	☐	1	2	3	1	2	3	4	5	1	2
(61) School assistance to students in transition from school to post-school life	☐	1	2	3	1	2	3	4	5	1	2
(62) Special education (IEPs)	☐	1	2	3	1	2	3	4	5	1	2
(63) Student attendance	☐	1	2	3	1	2	3	4	5	1	2
(64) Student discipline	☐	1	2	3	1	2	3	4	5	1	2
(65) Student testing program	☐	1	2	3	1	2	3	4	5	1	2

24. Mark the practice which *best* describes how your salary is determined.

(01) By the board, without consultation or negotiation.
(02) By the board, based upon superintendent's recommendation, without consultation or negotiation.
(03) By the superintendent, without consultation or negotiation.
(04) Through informal and individual negotiations with the board.
(05) Through informal and individual negotiations with the superintendent.
(06) Through informal negotiations with the board as a member of a group of administrators.
(07) Through informal negotiations with the superintendent as a member of a group of administrators.
(08) As a member of a formal bargaining group.
(09) Other: _____

25. Regardless of schedule of payment, what is your yearly salary based upon?

(01) 9 or 9½ months
(02) 10 or 10½ months
(03) 11 or 11½ months
(04) 12 months

26. Is your contract a multi-year contract?

(01) No.
(02) Yes—Two year contract.
(03) Yes—Three year contract.
(04) Yes—More than a three year contract.

27. In addition to your salary, which of the following fringe benefits do you receive from your school or district? *Circle all appropriate responses.*

    (01) No fringe benefits
    (02) Automobile or mileage allowance
    (03) College/University tuition for yourself
    (04) Dental insurance
    (05) Expense account
    (06) Housing or equivalent subsidy
    (07) Life insurance
    (08) Meals
    (09) Medical insurance
    (10) Retirement
    (11) Tuition for dependents (nonpublic school)

28. Do you have tenure *as principal?*   (01) Yes   (02) No

29. What is your perception of the importance of the following elements as they contributed to your first appointment to the principalship? Check to what degree they influenced that appointment.

	Very Important	Important	Of Some Importance	Of Little or No Importance
(01) Amount and quality of professional preparation				
(02) Assessment Center report				
(03) Contacts outside of the profession				
(04) Contacts within the profession				
(05) I was at the right spot at the right time				
(06) Number of years of teaching experience				
(07) Number of years as assistant principal				
(08) Performance on competitive exams				
(09) Success as a teacher				
(10) Success as an assistant principal				
(11) Successful job interview				
(12) The superintendent wanted me				
(13) Others, please specify: _____				
(14) _____				

30. In which of the following positions have you had one full year or more of experience? *Circle all that are appropriate.*

    (01) Athletic coach
    (02) Athletic director
    (03) Counselor or other guidance position
    (04) Dean or registrar
    (05) Department or area chairperson

31. Check to what degree the circumstances listed below affected your decisions to change or not change school districts?

	An Important Factor	Of Moderate Importance	Of Little or No Importance
(01) Family commitment (i.e., number of children, nearness of relatives) motivated me to pass up or not to seek opportunities in other communities or districts			
(02) Desire to live in a certain part of the country made me more place-oriented than career-oriented			
(03) The school environment (e.g., student discipline, parental views on education) has always been an important factor in my selection of jobs.			
(04) Job security, seniority, and retirement benefits outweigh the advantages that might ensue from changing school districts.			
(05) Other factors that have influenced your career mobility. Please specify: _____ _____			

32. Please rate your degree of satisfaction with your job environment as a principal.

Satisfaction with:	Very Satisfied	Satisfied	Dissatisfied
(01) The realization of expectations you had when you took the job?			
(02) The amount of time that you devote to the job?			
(03) The results that you achieve?			
(04) The salary you receive?			
(05) The working conditions?			
(06) The amount of assistance you receive from your immediate superior(s)?			
(07) The rapport that you have with teachers?			
(08) The rapport that you have with students?			
(09) The rapport that you have with parents/community?			

33. What is your career plan for the next 3-5 years? *Select one.*

(01) Remain in my present position.
(02) Retirement.
(03) Seek a position as superintendent.
(04) Seek a central office position other than the superintendency.
(05) Seek a different position as a high school principal.
(06) Seek a position as an elementary or middle level school principal.
(07) Seek a position in a junior/community college or university.
(08) Seek a position in a state department of education or other type of educational service agency (other than a school district).
(09) Return to full time teaching.
(10) Seek a position in a career field other than education. Please specify: _____
(11) I am undecided.

34. If you could choose again, would you select educational administration as a career?

(01) Yes—definitely   (03) Uncertain   (04) No—probably not
(02) Yes—probably   (05) No—definitely not

86

35. Below is a list of activities, grouped by categories, in which school administrators have reported personal involvement. Please rate *your own* involvement during the **current and past school year** by checking the appropriate space after each activity.

	Already well established involvement	Strong new initiatives	Moderate new initiatives	Little or no activity
Instruction				
(01) Clarification of instructional goals and priorities				
(02) Diagnosis of student learning styles				
(03) Monitoring of student progress, e.g., competency testing, outcomes-based education				
(04) Recognition of student academic achievement				
(05) Steps to enhance instructional standards and expectations				
(06) Steps to minimize interruptions of classes and instructional activities				
(07) Updating of curriculum and instructional resources				
(08) Others: _____				
Instructional Staff				
(09) Direct supervision and consultation				
(10) Evaluation of instruction				
(11) Inservice education				
(12) Involvement in curriculum development				
(13) Involvement in planning for instructional improvement				
(14) Involvement in school policy development				
(15) Teacher incentives, e.g., career ladders, released time, etc.				
(16) Others: _____				
Students and Student Relations				
(17) Activities to recognize student achievements and enhance student attitudes				
(18) Improvement of counseling services and procedures				
(19) Involvement in school policy making and problem solving				
(20) Review of attendance policies and procedures				
(21) Review of discipline rules and procedures				
(22) Others: _____				

	Already well established involvement	Strong new initiatives	Moderate new initiatives	Little or no activity
Administrative/Central Office				
(23) Improved administrative operations, e.g., use of computers, non-instructional staff				
(24) Involvement in long range planning				
(25) Preparation of proposals and recommendations for school improvement, e.g., articulation with other schools				
(26) Recommended changes in school operations and procedures, e.g., schedule of school day, student progress reporting				
(27) Others: _____				
Parent/Community Relations				
(28) Parent conferencing				
(29) Parent/community volunteers and aides in the school				
(30) Parental/community participation in policy making and problem solving				
(31) Strategies for improved communication, e.g., contacts with those who have no children in school				
(32) Use of community facilities and resources				
(33) Others: _____				
Innovative Programs (Please list and rate) (34)				
(35)				
(36)				

For the next five questions, circle the number on line A which describes your perception of how your job *actually is;* circle the number on line B to describe how you think your job *should be.*

36. A. How much prestige do you feel your position as principal *provides* in the community where your school is located?

1	2	3	4	5
Little		Moderate		Much

B. How much prestige do you feel your position as principal *should* provide you in the community where your school is located?

1	2	3	4	5
Little		Moderate		Much

37. A. How much opportunity for independent thought and action *does* your position as principal provide?

1	2	3	4	5
Little		Moderate		Much

B. How much opportunity for independent thought and action *should* your position as principal provide?

1	2	3	4	5
Littlo		Moderate		Much

38. A. How much self-fulfillment (i.e., the feeling of being able to use one's unique capabilities or realizing one's potential) *does* your position as principal provide?

1	2	3	4	5
Little		Moderate		Much

B. How much self-fulfillment *should* your position as principal provide?

1	2	3	4	5
Little		Moderate		Much

39. A. How much job security do you feel you *have* as a principal?

1	2	3	4	5
Little		Moderate		Much

B. How much job security do you feel you *should* have as a principal?

1	2	3	4	5
Little		Moderate		Much

40. A. How much opportunity to be helpful to other people *does* your position as principal provide?

1	2	3	4	5
Little		Moderate		Much

B. How much opportunity to be helpful to other people *should* your position as principal provide?

1	2	3	4	5
Little		Moderate		Much

In your opinion, which of the statements in the following three questions best characterize the role of the principal? *Circle only one answer for each question.*

41. Choose *one*
   (01) The principal primarily should represent the interests of parents, leaders, and patrons of the school.
   (02) The principal should take initiative in developing and implementing school policy according to his/her best professional judgment.

42. Choose *one*
   (01) The principal should effectively and efficiently manage the day-to-day affairs of the school.
   (02) The principal should lead the school in new educational directions according to his/her best professional judgment.

43. Choose *one*
   (01) The principal should play the major role in establishing the agenda and deciding the important issues in the school.
   (02) The principal should share decision making with the faculty on important school issues.

44. Below is a list of conditions or developments which many believe have a general influence upon secondary education. Please indicate how you feel each will influence *your* school during the *next three to five years.*

Check the appropriate space to indicate whether the condition or development will have (1) no influence, (2) some influence, or (3) strong influence on your school:

Condition	Strong Influence	Some Influence	No Influence
(01) Accountability movement			
(02) Alcohol abuse			
(03) Attention to academic achievement			
(04) Change in government funding			
(05) Changing family structure			
(06) Child abuse (physical, sexual)			
(07) Community participation			
(08) Community-based learning			
(09) Competency testing of students			
(10) Demand for basics			
(11) Drug abuse			
(12) Enrollment decline			
(13) Enrollment increase			
(14) Finance and general economy			
(15) Graduation requirements			
(16) New technologies			
(17) Personalized/effective education movement			
(18) Student attendance problems			
(19) Student motivation			
(20) Teacher competency			
(21) Teacher incentives			
(22) Teacher motivation			
(23) Teacher shortage			
(24) Teen emotional/psychological problems (runaways, suicide, etc.)			
(25) Teen sexual activity			
(26) Youth gang activity			
(27) Youth unemployment			
(28) Other: _____			

90

NATIONAL ASSOCIATION OF SECONDARY SCHOOL PRINCIPALS

Reston, Virginia 22091

A National Study of High School Leaders and Their Schools

SURVEY OF HIGH SCHOOL PRINCIPALS

Form B

DIRECTIONS

Your questionnaire is identified by the label placed on it. It is not necessary to sign or place your name on the questionnaire. In reporting results, only statistical summaries of the responses of groups of principals will be cited. In no case will the identity of an individual be divulged. You are urged to make every answer a sincere one.

Circle the number of the appropriate response using pen or pencil. If you change a response, please make the change distinctly so there is no doubt about how you wish to answer.

Attempt to answer every question. For some questions none of the alternatives may correspond exactly to your situation or to the opinion you hold. In such cases mark the alternative which comes closest to the answer you would like to give.

Place your completed questionnaire in the envelope provided and mail it to NASSP. Thank you for your cooperation and assistance in this important study.

••

Advisory Committee for A Study of High School Leaders and Their Schools:

Patricia D. Campbell, Lakewood High School, Lakewood, Colorado; Glen M. DeHaven, Oldtown School, Oldtown, Maryland; Richard Gorton, School of Education, University of Wisconsin–Milwaukee; Jacqueline H. Simmons, Paul Robeson High School, Chicago, Illinois; Norman O. Stevens, Mill River Union High School, North Clarendon, Vermont; Michael K. Thomas, Vashon High School, St. Louis, Missouri; Peggy Walters, J. Frank Dobie High School, Houston, Texas; Gary P. Wells, Henley High School, Klamath Falls, Oregon; Jeannette Wheatley, Cass Technical High School, Detroit, Michigan; James V. Wright, Fremont Ross High School, Fremont, Ohio.

Research Team:

Lorin W. Anderson, University of South Carolina; Edgar A. Kelley, Western Michigan University; Lloyd E. McCleary, University of Utah; Leonard O. Pellicer, University of South Carolina; James W. Keefe, NASSP

1. What is your sex?   (01) Male   (02) Female

2. What is your age?

(01) 23 or under   (04) 35-39   (07) 50-54
(02) 24-29   (05) 40-44   (08) 55-59
(03) 30-34   (06) 45-49   (09) 60 or older

3. With which ethnic group would you identify yourself?

(01) White   (03) Hispanic   (05) Asian
(02) Black   (04) American Indian   (06) Other: _____

4. In which of the following areas did you major as an *undergraduate*? *Select only one answer.*

(01) Secondary education (other than physical education)
(02) Physical education
(03) Elementary education
(04) Humanities (literature, languages, etc.)
(05) Physical or biological sciences
(06) Social sciences (sociology, history, etc.)
(07) Mathematics
(08) Fine arts
(09) Business
(10) Vocational-Technical (home economics, industrial arts, etc.)
(11) Other: _____

5. What is the highest degree you have earned?

(01) Less than a BA
(02) Bachelor's Degree
(03) Master's Degree in Education
(04) Master's Degree not in Education
(05) Master's Degree plus some additional graduate work
(06) Educational Specialist, six-year program or equivalent
(07) Master's Degree plus *all course work* for a doctorate
(08) Doctor of Education
(09) Doctor of Philosophy
(10) Other: _____

6. How many years of *teaching* experience, regardless of level, did you have prior to taking your present position? Do not include years as a full-time administrator, supervisor, counselor, psychologist, or librarian.

(01) None   (04) 4-6 years   (07) 15-19 years
(02) One year   (05) 7-9 years   (08) 20-24 years
(03) 2-3 years   (06) 10-14 years   (09) 25 or more years

7. What was the last position you held prior to becoming a high school principal? *Select only one answer.*

(01) Teacher
(02) Assistant principal of an elementary or middle level school
(03) Assistant principal of a high school
(04) Principal of an elementary or middle level school
(05) Guidance counselor
(06) Other—education, specify: _____
(07) Other—non-education, specify: _____

8. At what age were you appointed to your first principalship?

(01) 23 or under   (04) 35-39   (07) 50-54
(02) 24-29   (05) 40-44   (08) 55-59
(03) 30-34   (06) 45-49   (09) 60 or older

9. How many years have you served as a principal, including this school year?

(01) One year
(02) 2-3 years
(03) 4-5 years

(04) 6-7 years
(05) 8-9 years
(06) 10-14 years

(07) 15-19 years
(08) 20-24 years
(09) 25 or more years

10. How long have you been a principal in this school, including this school year?

(01) One year
(02) Two years
(03) Three years

(04) 4-5 years
(05) 6-8 years
(06) 9-11 years

(07) 12-14 years
(08) 15-17 years
(09) 18 or more years

11. Which of the following categories best describes the school of which you are principal? *Choose only one answer.*

(01) Public comprehensive
(02) Public "alternative"
(03) Public special (commercial, vocational, arts, etc.)
(04) Parochial or diocesan

(05) Private, religious affiliated
(06) Private, not religious affiliated
(07) Other, specify _____

12. What grades are included in your school?

(01) Kindergarten-12
(02) 1-12
(03) 7-12
(04) 8-12

(05) 9-12
(06) 10-12
(07) 11-12
(08) Other, specify _____

13. How many high school students (grade 9 and above) were enrolled in your school on October 1st of the current school year?

(01) Fewer than 250
(02) 250-499
(03) 500-749

(04) 750-999
(05) 1,000-1,499
(06) 1,500-1,999

(07) 2,000-2,499
(08) 2,500 or more

14. In which geographic region is your school located?

(01) New England
(02) Mid-Atlantic
(03) South

(04) Midwest
(05) Southwest
(06) Inter Mountain

(07) West Coast
(08) Non-contiguous
(09) Other, specify _____

15. What is the average per-student expenditure for each high school student in your school for the current school year (exclusive of capital outlay)?

(01) Less than $1,500
(02) 1,500-1,999
(03) 2,000-2,499

(04) 2,500-2,999
(05) 3,000-3,499
(06) 3,500-3,999

(07) 4,000-4,499
(08) 4,500-4,999
(09) 5,000 or more

16. Which of the following population categories best describes the locale of the high school in which you are principal?

(01) City, more than 1,000,000
(02) City, 150,000-999,999
(03) Suburban, related to city of 150,000 or more

(04) City, 25,000-149,999, distinct from a metropolitan area
(05) City, 5,000-24,999, not suburban
(06) Town or rural under 5,000

17. What would you estimate is the percent of average daily attendance of those enrolled in your school for the current school year?

(01) Less than 50%
(02) 50% to 70%

(03) 71% to 80%
(04) 81% to 90%

(05) 91% to 95%
(06) 96% or more

18. What percentage of all pupils who enter the first year at your school drop out before graduation? Do not include those who transfer to another school.

(01) Less than 5%
(02) 5% to 9%
(03) 10% to 19%

(04) 20% to 29%
(05) 30% to 39%
(06) 40% to 59%

(07) 60% to 79%
(08) 80% to 99%

19. What percentage of the students in your current graduating class are college bound?

(01) Less than 5%   (04) 20% to 29%   (07) 60% to 79%
(02) 5% to 9%   (05) 30% to 39%   (08) 80% to 94%
(03) 10% to 19%   (06) 40% to 59%   (09) 95% or more

20. What is your current annual salary as principal? Do not include fringe benefits.

(01) Less than $25,000   (04) 35,000-39,999   (07) 50,000-54,999
(02) 25,000-29,999   (05) 40,000-44,999   (08) 55,000-59,999
(03) 30,000-34,999   (06) 45,000-49,999   (09) 60,000 or more
                                                         (10) Not applicable (religious order)

21. On the average, how many hours a week do you work at your job as principal?

(01) Less than 40   (03) 45-49   (05) 55-59
(02) 40-44   (04) 50-54   (06) 60 or more

22. How do you spend your time during the typical work week? Rank these nine areas according to the amount of time spent in each area.

In Column A, mark a "1" next to the area in which you *do spend* the most time, ranking all areas until you have marked a "9" next to the area in which you spend the least time.

Then, in Column B, mark a "1" next to the area in which you feel you *should spend* the most time, ranking all items accordingly until you have marked a "9" next to the area in which you feel you should spend the least time.

A. DO Spend Time	Area of Responsibility	SHOULD Spend Time
_____	(01) *Program Development* (curriculum, instructional leadership, etc.)	_____
_____	(02) *Personnel* (evaluating, advising, conferring, recruiting, etc.)	_____
_____	(03) *Management* (weekly calendar, office, budget, memos, etc.)	_____
_____	(04) *Student Activities* (meetings, supervision, planning, etc.)	_____
_____	(05) *Student Behavior* (discipline, attendance, meetings, etc.)	_____
_____	(06) *Community* (PTA, advisory groups, parent conferences, etc.)	_____
_____	(07) *District Office* (meetings, task forces, reports, etc.)	_____
_____	(08) *Professional Development* (reading, conferences, etc.)	_____
_____	(09) *Planning* (annual, long range)	_____

94

23. **Duties and Responsibilities of Assistant Principals.** Principals have final responsibility for everything that happens in a school, but assistant principals share in differing degrees in that responsibility. Please indicate the job profile of the assistant principal(s) in your school in the following chart. Please check the "not applicable" box for any function that does not apply.

Directions:

RESPONSIBILITY	IMPORTANCE	DISCRETIONARY BEHAVIOR
In the appropriate column, indicate the **degree of responsibility** assistant principals have for each duty delegated. Circle the number: (01) Slight —The principal does the job. APs may aid at his direction. (02) Shared—Delegated with close supervision; principal and assistant principals work together. (03) Full —Delegated with general supervision; assistant principals are held responsible for the job.	In the appropriate column, indicate the **degree of importance** you believe the **delegated** duty has to the proper functioning of the school. Circle the number: (01) Least importance (02) Minor importance (03) Average importance (04) Major importance (05) Most importance	In the appropriate column, indicate your judgment of the **level of discretionary** behavior involved in the completion of any **delegated** duty in **your** school. (A duty may be of relatively minor importance and yet it could involve high discretionary behavior. The reverse may be equally true.) Circle the number: (01) Low —Behavior that is directed in large measure by others; behavior that involves restricted high order decision making. (02) High —Behavior that is self-directing, involving high order decision making.

		SAMPLE RESPONSES									
Illustrated Examples	NOT APPLICABLE	Degree of Responsibility			Degree of Importance					Level of Discretionary Behavior	
		SLIGHT	SHARED	FULL	LEAST	MINOR	AVERAGE	MAJOR	MOST	LOW	HIGH
Responsibility for:											
01 Faculty Socials	☐	1	2	③	1	②	3	4	5	1	②
02 "Career day" conferences	☐	①	2	3	1	2	3	④	5	①	2
03 Report card procedures	☑	1	2	3	1	2	3	4	5	1	2

95

	NOT APPLICABLE	Degree of Responsibility			Degree of Importance					Level of Discretionary Behavior	
Circle Appropriate Code Numbers (For an item that is not applicable to your school situation, place a check (✔) in the NA box after the item).		SLIGHT	SHARED	FULL	LEAST	MINOR	AVERAGE	MAJOR	MOST	LOW	HIGH

Responsibility for:

Curriculum and Instruction

	NA	SLIGHT	SHARED	FULL	LEAST	MINOR	AVERAGE	MAJOR	MOST	LOW	HIGH
(01) Articulation with feeder schools	☐	1	2	3	1	2	3	4	5	1	2
(02) Curriculum development	☐	1	2	3	1	2	3	4	5	1	2
(03) Evaluation of teachers	☐	1	2	3	1	2	3	4	5	1	2
(04) Innovations, experiments, and research	☐	1	2	3	1	2	3	4	5	1	2
(05) Instructional media and materials	☐	1	2	3	1	2	3	4	5	1	2
(06) Instructional methods	☐	1	2	3	1	2	3	4	5	1	2
(07) Instructional software	☐	1	2	3	1	2	3	4	5	1	2
(08) School-wide examinations	☐	1	2	3	1	2	3	4	5	1	2
(09) School master schedule	☐	1	2	3	1	2	3	4	5	1	2
(10) Staff inservice	☐	1	2	3	1	2	3	4	5	1	2
(11) Textbook selection	☐	1	2	3	1	2	3	4	5	1	2
(12) Work-study program	☐	1	2	3	1	2	3	4	5	1	2

Responsibility for:

Community Relations

	NA	SLIGHT	SHARED	FULL	LEAST	MINOR	AVERAGE	MAJOR	MOST	LOW	HIGH
(13) Administrative representative at community functions	☐	1	2	3	1	2	3	4	5	1	2
(14) Adult education program	☐	1	2	3	1	2	3	4	5	1	2
(15) Coordinating community resources for instruction	☐	1	2	3	1	2	3	4	5	1	2
(16) Informing public of school achievements	☐	1	2	3	1	2	3	4	5	1	2
(17) Liaison with community youth-serving agencies	☐	1	2	3	1	2	3	4	5	1	2
(18) Parent-Teacher Association	☐	1	2	3	1	2	3	4	5	1	2
(19) School alumni association	☐	1	2	3	1	2	3	4	5	1	2
(20) School public relations program	☐	1	2	3	1	2	3	4	5	1	2
(21) School participation in community fund drives	☐	1	2	3	1	2	3	4	5	1	2

Responsibility for:

School Management

	NA	SLIGHT	SHARED	FULL	LEAST	MINOR	AVERAGE	MAJOR	MOST	LOW	HIGH
(22) Building use—nonschool-related	☐	1	2	3	1	2	3	4	5	1	2
(23) Building use—school-related	☐	1	2	3	1	2	3	4	5	1	2
(24) Cafeteria services	☐	1	2	3	1	2	3	4	5	1	2
(25) Clerical services	☐	1	2	3	1	2	3	4	5	1	2
(26) Computer services	☐	1	2	3	1	2	3	4	5	1	2
(27) Custodial services	☐	1	2	3	1	2	3	4	5	1	2

Circle Appropriate Code Numbers (For an item that is not applicable to your school situation, place a check (✔) in the NA box after the item).	NOT APPLICABLE	Degree of Responsibility			Degree of Importance					Level of Discretionary Behavior	
		SLIGHT	SHARED	FULL	LEAST	MINOR	AVERAGE	MAJOR	MOST	LOW	HIGH
(28) Emergency arrangements	☐	1	2	3	1	2	3	4	5	1	2
(29) Graduation activities	☐	1	2	3	1	2	3	4	5	1	2
(30) Noninstructional equipment and supplies	☐	1	2	3	1	2	3	4	5	1	2
(31) School budget	☐	1	2	3	1	2	3	4	5	1	2
(32) School calendars	☐	1	2	3	1	2	3	4	5	1	2
(33) School daily bulletins	☐	1	2	3	1	2	3	4	5	1	2
(34) School financial accounts	☐	1	2	3	1	2	3	4	5	1	2
(35) School policies	☐	1	2	3	1	2	3	4	5	1	2
(36) Special arrangements at start and close of school year	☐	1	2	3	1	2	3	4	5	1	2
(37) Transportation services	☐	1	2	3	1	2	3	4	5	1	2

Responsibility for:

Staff Personnel

(38) Faculty meetings	☐	1	2	3	1	2	3	4	5	1	2
(39) Orientation program for new teachers	☐	1	2	3	1	2	3	4	5	1	2
(40) Student teachers	☐	1	2	3	1	2	3	4	5	1	2
(41) Substitute teachers	☐	1	2	3	1	2	3	4	5	1	2
(42) Teacher "duty" rosters	☐	1	2	3	1	2	3	4	5	1	2
(43) Teacher personnel records	☐	1	2	3	1	2	3	4	5	1	2
(44) Teacher incentives, motivation	☐	1	2	3	1	2	3	4	5	1	2
(45) Teacher selection	☐	1	2	3	1	2	3	4	5	1	2

Responsibility for:

Student Activities

(46) Assemblies	☐	1	2	3	1	2	3	4	5	1	2
(47) Athletic program	☐	1	2	3	1	2	3	4	5	1	2
(48) School club program	☐	1	2	3	1	2	3	4	5	1	2
(49) School dances	☐	1	2	3	1	2	3	4	5	1	2
(50) School newspaper	☐	1	2	3	1	2	3	4	5	1	2
(51) School traffic or safety squad	☐	1	2	3	1	2	3	4	5	1	2
(52) Student council	☐	1	2	3	1	2	3	4	5	1	2
(53) Student photographs	☐	1	2	3	1	2	3	4	5	1	2
(54) Student store	☐	1	2	3	1	2	3	4	5	1	2

Responsibility for:

Student Services

(55) Financial aid for students	☐	1	2	3	1	2	3	4	5	1	2
(56) Guidance program	☐	1	2	3	1	2	3	4	5	1	2
(57) Instruction for home-bound students	☐	1	2	3	1	2	3	4	5	1	2

Circle Appropriate Code Numbers (For an item that is not applicable to your school situation, place a check (✓) in the NA box after the item).	NOT APPLICABLE	Degree of Responsibility			Degree of Importance					Level of Discretionary Behavior	
		SLIGHT	SHARED	FULL	LEAST	MINOR	AVERAGE	MAJOR	MOST	LOW	HIGH
(58) Medical, dental, and health services	☐	1	2	3	1	2	3	4	5	1	2
(59) Orientation program for new students	☐	1	2	3	1	2	3	4	5	1	2
(60) Relationships with educational and employer representatives	☐	1	2	3	1	2	3	4	5	1	2
(61) School assistance to students in transition from school to post-school life	☐	1	2	3	1	2	3	4	5	1	2
(62) Special education (IEPs)	☐	1	2	3	1	2	3	4	5	1	2
(63) Student attendance	☐	1	2	3	1	2	3	4	5	1	2
(64) Student discipline	☐	1	2	3	1	2	3	4	5	1	2
(65) Student testing program	☐	1	2	3	1	2	3	4	5	1	2

24. In how many civic and political organizations (Chamber of Commerce, Rotary, etc.) do you hold active membership?

(01) None
(02) One
(03) Two
(04) Three
(05) Four
(06) Five or more

25. Circle each type of professional development activity in which you have been involved during the last two years.

(01) National professional organization institute or conference (voluntary participation).
(02) State professional organization activity (voluntary participation).
(03) Activity conducted by private consultants at an out-of-district location (voluntary participation).
(04) District activity required as part of employment.
(05) Other district activities (voluntary participation).
(06) Enrollment in graduate courses at an institution of higher education.
(07) State department of education or county agency activity (voluntary participation).
(08) State department of education or county agency activity (required participation).
(09) Principal Center or Academy (voluntary participation).
(10) Other, specify: _____

26. In how many professional educational organizations do you hold active membership at the state or national level? (Count an organization and its affiliates, such as NASSP and its state affiliates, only once.)

(01) NASSP and its affiliates.
(02) NASSP and one other professional education organization.
(03) NASSP and two other professional education organizations.
(04) NASSP and three other professional education organizations.
(05) Other organizations but not NASSP and affiliates.

98

27. Circle all of the following that apply to your district's support for your participation in the activities of professional educational organizations.

    My district:

    (01) Discourages active participation in professional organizations.
    (02) Encourages active participation at my personal expense.
    (03) Pays my membership dues.
    (04) Allows released time to attend meetings/conferences.
    (05) Pays a portion (half or less) of my expenses to attend meetings/conferences.
    (06) Pays all or most of my expenses to attend meetings/conferences.

28. Do you teach any regularly scheduled classes?
    (01) No   (02) Yes—one course   (03) Yes, two or three courses

For this question, please circle the number which best describes your perception of the amount and quality of your administrative staff.

29. A. The *amount* of administrative assistance in my building is:

1	2	3	4	5
Inadequate		Adequate		More than adequate

  B. The *quality* of administrative assistance in my building is:

1	2	3	4	5
Inadequate		Adequate		More than adequate

30. Who assigns the duties and responsibilities of assistant principals in your school?
    (01) Principal alone
    (02) Superintendent alone
    (03) School board alone
    (04) Principal in conference with assistant principal
    (05) Principal in conference with superintendent and assistant principal
    (06) Principal in conference with superintendent, school board, and assistant principal
    (07) Principal and superintendent
    (08) Principal and school board
    (09) Principal with superintendent and school board
    (10) Superintendent and school board
    (11) Other, please specify _____

31. Which of the following best describes your district's legal status on collective bargaining? *Choose only one answer.*

    (01) No collective bargaining.
    (02) Collective bargaining with teachers only.
    (03) Collective bargaining with administrators only.
    (04) Collective bargaining with teachers *and* administrators.
    (05) Collective bargaining with all employees.

32. Which of the following best describes collective bargaining's impact upon your relationships with others? *Circle all that are appropriate.*

    (01) No collective bargaining.
    (02) Enhanced my relationships with central office personnel.
    (03) Caused my relationships with central office personnel to deteriorate.
    (04) No appreciable effect on my relationships with central office personnel.
    (05) Enhanced my relationships with teachers.
    (06) Caused my relationships with teachers to deteriorate.
    (07) No appreciable effect on my relationships with teachers.

33. To what extent do you participate in determining the budget allocation for your school?

    (01) High participation   (03) Little participation
    (02) Moderate participation   (04) No participation

34. To what extent do you have the authority to approve the allocation of discretionary funds within your school budget; i.e., how much autonomy or latitude do you have in the allocation of monies which are available to your building?

(01) Unrestricted authority
(02) Authority with some restriction
(03) Little authority
(04) No authority

35. How much authority do you have to fill teacher vacancies? *Select one.*

(01) I make the selection and the central office endorses it.
(02) I make the selection within limited options stipulated by the central office.
(03) I recommend a person to fill the vacancy and the central office makes the decision.
(04) The central office selects the teacher to fill the vacancy.

36. How much authority do you have to make personnel decisions such as employing one full-time teacher or an alternative; e.g., two or three teacher aides?

(01) Unrestricted authority
(02) Authority with some restriction
(03) Little authority
(04) No authority

37. How many instructional staff members are there in your school (include teachers, counselors, media specialists, instructional aides)?

(01) Fewer than 20
(02) 20-39
(03) 40-59
(04) 60-79
(05) 80-99
(06) 100-119
(07) 120-139
(08) 140 or more

38. What percentage of your full-time teachers are men?

(01) Less than 10%
(02) 10-19%
(03) 20-29%
(04) 30-39%
(05) 40-49%
(06) 50-59%
(07) 60-69%
(08) 70-79%
(09) 80-89%
(10) 90-100%

39. Please indicate the approximate percentage of teachers with the types of instructional assignments described below. Express in percent multiples of 5. Your responses should total 100%.

_____ (01) Percentage of teachers with one subject preparation.
_____ (02) Percentage of teachers with two subject preparations.
_____ (03) Percentage of teachers with three subject preparations.
_____ (04) Percentage of teachers with four or more subject preparations.

40. Please circle the *three* most important skills and characteristics of a "good" teacher.
(01) Competence in subject matter knowledge.
(02) Competence in methods of instruction.
(03) Competence in adjusting instruction to the varying learning styles and learning skills of the students.
(04) Competence in helping students acquire basic learning outcomes.
(05) Competence in developing and evaluating new instructional techniques.
(06) Interpersonal skills in working with colleagues.
(07) Interpersonal skills in working with students.
(08) Interpersonal skills in working with parents and citizens.
(09) Sensitivity to differing socioeconomic backgrounds of students.
(10) Sensitivity to differing cultural backgrounds of students.
(11) Skill in developing positive student self-concept.
(12) Skill in developing in students respect for others.
(13) Ability to model appropriate adult behaviors.
(14) Good employee behaviors and work habits (dependability, punctuality, attendance, completion of tasks on time).

41. What is the role of the homeroom/homebase teacher in your school? Circle only *one* answer.

(01) No such role
(02) Attendance only
(03) Attendance and other administrative functions
(04) Advisement (Adviser/advisee, Teacher adviser)
(05) Guidance functions in addition to advisement

42. Much is written about involving parents and the community in the school. Circle the areas below in which you feel parents/community should be involved in your school.

(01) Curriculum development
(02) Development of rules and procedures for student discipline
(03) Evaluation of curriculum or instruction
(04) Evaluation of school or classroom climate
(05) Evaluation of school personnel
(06) Fund raising for a school-based foundation
(07) Fund raising for individual school projects
(08) Instructional assistance in the classrooms
(09) Review and evaluation of instructional materials
(10) Selection of school personnel
(11) Student activity program planning
(12) Supervision of student activities
(13) Volunteer services for general administrative tasks
(14) Review committees for appeals on student rights and responsibilities
(15) Review and evaluation of school grading and reporting practices

43. Below are several kinds of individuals or groups external to the school, which may have sought, successfully or unsuccessfully, to bring about changes in your school. Check the extent of influence of each interest group on your school during the past **two** years.

	Little/No Influence	Moderate Influence	Extreme Influence
(01) Athletic boosters (especially alumni)			
(02) Band/Music boosters			
(03) Business community			
(04) Censorship groups (books, programs, etc.)			
(05) Citizen or parent groups (non-PTA)			
(06) Extremist individuals or groups (right or left)			
(07) Individuals/Groups concerned about national reports, school reform			
(08) Individuals/Groups concerned about testing			
(09) Legal aid groups			
(10) Local elementary schools			
(11) Local middle level schools			
(12) Local labor organizations			
(13) Local media			
(14) PTA or PTO			
(15) Religious or church individuals/groups			
(16) State colleges and/or universities			
(17) Teachers' organizations			
(18) Womens' or minority rights organizations			

44. Listed below are several factors which could be considered "roadblocks" preventing principals from doing the job they would like to do. Indicate by checking the appropriate boxes whether each factor has or has not been a roadblock to you as principal during the past *two years*.

	Not a Factor	Somewhat a Factor	Serious Factor
(01) Collective bargaining agreement			
(02) Defective communication among administrative levels			
(03) Inability to obtain funding			
(04) Inability to provide teacher time for planning or professional development			
(05) Insufficient space and physical facilities			
(06) Lack of competent administrative assistance			
(07) Lack of competent office help			
(08) Lack of district-wide flexibility (all schools conform to same policy)			
(09) Lack of content knowledge among staff			
(10) Lack of opportunity to select staff			
(11) Lack of time for myself			
(12) Long-standing tradition(s) in the school/district			
(13) New state guidelines/requirements			
(14) Parents apathetic or irresponsible about their children			
(15) Pressure from community			
(16) Problem students (apathetic, hostile, etc.)			
(17) Resistance to change by staff			
(18) Superintendent or central office staff who have not measured up to expectations			
(19) Teacher shortage			
(20) Teacher tenure			
(21) Teacher turnover			
(22) Time required to administer, supervise student activities			
(23) Time taken by administrative detail at expense of more important matters			
(24) Too large a student body			
(25) Too small a student body			
(26) Variations in the ability and dedication of staff			

102

45. Circle each response below which represents a use of computers, data processing equipment, or other technological services in your school.

   (01) To schedule classes
   (02) To prepare grade reports
   (03) To maintain student records on attendance
   (04) To maintain student records on disciplinary behaviors
   (05) To maintain personnel records
   (06) To select samples for student surveys
   (07) To select samples for surveys of parents and citizens
   (08) As an interactive communication device with other professionals
   (09) As an interactive communication device to identify and retrieve materials for instruction
   (10) To maintain fiscal records
   (11) To prepare written communications such as brochures, newsletters, etc.
   (12) As basic equipment for office personnel
   (13) As part of the library/media center operations of the school
   (14) To provide a "hot-line" information service for persons who call the school
   (15) To provide computer-based telephone messages to the home (e.g., to notify of student absences)
   (16) To assist teachers in developing tests
   (17) To score teacher-made tests
   (18) Other—Please specify: _____
   _____
   _____

In your opinion, which of the statements in the following three questions best characterize the role of the principal? *Circle only one answer for each question.*

46. Choose *one*

   (01) The principal primarily should represent the interests of parents, leaders, and patrons of the school.
   (02) The principal should take initiative in developing and implementing school policy according to his/her best professional judgment.

47. Choose *one*

   (01) The principal should effectively and efficiently manage the day-to-day affairs of the school.
   (02) The principal should lead the school in new educational directions according to his/her best professional judgment.

48. Choose *one*

   (01) The principal should play the major role in establishing the agenda and deciding the important issues in the school.
   (02) The principal should share decision making with the faculty on important school issues.

49. Below is a list of conditions or developments which many believe have a general influence upon secondary education. Please indicate how you feel each will influence *your* school during the *next three to five years.*

Check the appropriate space to indicate whether the condition or development will have (1) no influence, (2) some influence, or (3) strong influence on your school.

Condition	No Influence	Some Influence	Strong Influence
(01) Accountability movement			
(02) Alcohol abuse			
(03) Attention to academic achievement			
(04) Change in government funding			
(05) Changing family structure			
(06) Child abuse (physical, sexual)			
(07) Community participation			
(08) Community-based learning			
(09) Competency testing of students			
(10) Demand for basics			
(11) Drug abuse			
(12) Enrollment decline			
(13) Enrollment increase			
(14) Finance and general economy			
(15) Graduation requirements			
(16) New technologies			
(17) Personalized/effective education movement			
(18) Student attendance problems			
(19) Student motivation			
(20) Teacher competency			
(21) Teacher incentives			
(22) Teacher motivation			
(23) Teacher shortage			
(24) Teen emotional/psychological problems (runaways, suicide, etc.)			
(25) Teen sexual activity			
(26) Youth gang activity			
(27) Youth unemployment			
(28) Other: _____			

104

NATIONAL ASSOCIATION OF SECONDARY SCHOOL PRINCIPALS

Reston, Virginia 22091

A National Study of High School Leaders and Their Schools

SURVEY OF HIGH SCHOOL PRINCIPALS
Form C

DIRECTIONS

Your questionnaire is identified by the label placed on it. It is not necessary to sign or place your name on the questionnaire. In reporting results, only statistical summaries of the responses of groups of principals will be cited. In no case will the identity of an individual be divulged. You are urged to make every answer a sincere one.

Circle the number of the appropriate response using pen or pencil. If you change a response, please make the change distinctly so there is no doubt about how you wish to answer.

Attempt to answer every question. For some questions none of the alternatives may correspond exactly to your situation or to the opinion you hold. In such cases mark the alternative which comes closest to the answer you would like to give.

Place your completed questionnaire in the envelope provided and mail it to NASSP. Thank you for your cooperation and assistance in this important study.

••

Advisory Committee for A Study of High School Leaders and Their Schools:

Patricia D. Campbell, Lakewood High School, Lakewood, Colorado; Glen M. DeHaven, Oldtown School, Oldtown, Maryland; Richard Gorton, School of Education, University of Wisconsin–Milwaukee; Jacqueline H. Simmons, Paul Robeson High School, Chicago, Illinois; Norman O. Stevens, Mill River Union High School, North Clarendon, Vermont; Michael K. Thomas, Vashon High School, St. Louis, Missouri; Peggy Walters, J. Frank Dobie High School, Houston, Texas; Gary P. Wells, Henley High School, Klamath Falls, Oregon; Jeannette Wheatley, Cass Technical High School, Detroit, Michigan; James V. Wright, Fremont Ross High School, Fremont, Ohio.

Research Team:

Lorin W. Anderson, University of South Carolina; Edgar A. Kelley, Western Michigan University; Lloyd E. McCleary, University of Utah; Leonard O. Pellicer, University of South Carolina; James W. Keefe, NASSP

105

1. What is your sex?   (01) Male   (02) Female

2. What is your age?

    (01) 23 or under   (04) 35-39   (07) 50-54
    (02) 24-29   (05) 40-44   (08) 55-59
    (03) 30-34   (06) 45-49   (09) 60 or older

3. With which ethnic group would you identify yourself?

    (01) White   (03) Hispanic   (05) Asian
    (02) Black   (04) American Indian   (06) Other: _____

4. In which of the following areas did you major as an *undergraduate? Select only one answer.*

    (01) Secondary education (other than physical education)
    (02) Physical education
    (03) Elementary education
    (04) Humanities (literature, languages, etc.)
    (05) Physical or biological sciences
    (06) Social sciences (sociology, history, etc.)
    (07) Mathematics
    (08) Fine arts
    (09) Business
    (10) Vocational-Technical (home economics, industrial arts, etc.)
    (11) Other: _____

5. What is the highest degree you have earned?

    (01) Less than a BA
    (02) Bachelor's Degree
    (03) Master's Degree in Education
    (04) Master's Degree not in Education
    (05) Master's Degree plus some additional graduate work
    (06) Educational Specialist, six-year program or equivalent
    (07) Master's Degree plus *all course work* for a doctorate
    (08) Doctor of Education
    (09) Doctor of Philosophy
    (10) Other: _____

6. How many years of *teaching* experience, regardless of level, did you have prior to taking your present position? Do not include years as a full-time administrator, supervisor, counselor, psychologist, or librarian.

    (01) None   (04) 4-6 years   (07) 15-19 years
    (02) One year   (05) 7-9 years   (08) 20-24 years
    (03) 2-3 years   (06) 10-14 years   (09) 25 or more years

7. What was the last position you held prior to becoming a high school principal? *Select only one answer.*

    (01) Teacher
    (02) Assistant principal of an elementary or middle level school
    (03) Assistant principal of a high school
    (04) Principal of an elementary or middle level school
    (05) Guidance counselor
    (06) Other—education, specify: _____
    (07) Other—non-education, specify: _____

8. At what age were you appointed to your first principalship?

    (01) 23 or under   (04) 35-39   (07) 50-54
    (02) 24-29   (05) 40-44   (08) 55-59
    (03) 30-34   (06) 45-49   (09) 60 or older

9. How many years have you served as a principal, including this school year?

(01) One year
(02) 2-3 years
(03) 4-5 years

(04) 6-7 years
(05) 8-9 years
(06) 10-14 years

(07) 15-19 years
(08) 20-24 years
(09) 25 or more years

10. How long have you been a principal in this school, including this school year?

(01) One year
(02) Two years
(03) Three years

(04) 4-5 years
(05) 6-8 years
(06) 9-11 years

(07) 12-14 years
(08) 15-17 years
(09) 18 or more years

11. Which of the following categories best describes the school of which you are principal? *Choose only one answer.*

(01) Public comprehensive
(02) Public "alternative"
(03) Public special (commercial, vocational, arts, etc.)
(04) Parochial or diocesan

(05) Private, religious affiliated
(06) Private, not religious affiliated
(07) Other, specify _____

12. What grades are included in your school?

(01) Kindergarten-12
(02) 1-12
(03) 7-12
(04) 8-12

(05) 9-12
(06) 10-12
(07) 11-12
(08) Other, specify _____

13. How many high school students (grade 9 and above) were enrolled in your school on October 1st of the current school year?

(01) Fewer than 250
(02) 250-499
(03) 500-749

(04) 750-999
(05) 1,000-1,499
(06) 1,500-1,999

(07) 2,000-2,499
(08) 2,500 or more

14. In which geographic region is your school located?

(01) New England
(02) Mid-Atlantic
(03) South

(04) Midwest
(05) Southwest
(06) Inter Mountain

(07) West Coast
(08) Non-contiguous
(09) Other, specify _____

15. What is the average per-student expenditure for each high school student in your school for the current school year (exclusive of capital outlay)?

(01) Less than $1,500
(02) 1,500-1,999
(03) 2,000-2,499

(04) 2,500-2,999
(05) 3,000-3,499
(06) 3,500-3,999

(07) 4,000-4,499
(08) 4,500-4,999
(09) 5,000 or more

16. Which of the following population categories best describes the locale of the high school in which you are principal?

(01) City, more than 1,000,000
(02) City, 150,000-999,999
(03) Suburban, related to city of 150,000 or more

(04) City, 25,000-149,999, distinct from a metropolitan area
(05) City, 5,000-24,999, not suburban
(06) Town or rural under 5,000

17. What would you estimate is the percent of average daily attendance of those enrolled in your school for the current school year?

(01) Less than 50%
(02) 50% to 70%

(03) 71% to 80%
(04) 81% to 90%

(05) 91% to 95%
(06) 96% or more

18. What percentage of all pupils who enter the first year at your school drop out before graduation? Do not include those who transfer to another school.

(01) Less than 5%
(02) 5% to 9%
(03) 10% to 19%

(04) 20% to 29%
(05) 30% to 39%
(06) 40% to 59%

(07) 60% to 79%
(08) 80% to 99%

19. What percentage of the students in your current graduating class are college bound?

(01) Less than 5%   (04) 20% to 29%   (07) 60% to 79%
(02) 5% to 9%   (05) 30% to 39%   (08) 80% to 94%
(03) 10% to 19%   (06) 40% to 59%   (09) 95% or more

20. What is your current annual salary as principal? Do not include fringe benefits.

(01) Less than $25,000   (04) 35,000-39,999   (07) 50,000-54,999
(02) 25,000-29,999   (05) 40,000-44,999   (08) 55,000-59,999
(03) 30,000-34,999   (06) 45,000-49,999   (09) 60,000 or more
                                                     (10) Not applicable (religious order)

21. On the average, how many hours a week do you work at your job as principal?

(01) Less than 40   (03) 45-49   (05) 55-59
(02) 40-44   (04) 50-54   (06) 60 or more

22. How do you spend your time during the typical work week? Rank these nine areas according to the amount of time spent in each area.

In Column A, mark a "1" next to the area in which you **do spend** the most time, ranking all areas until you have marked a "9" next to the area in which you spend the least time.

Then, in Column B, mark a "1" next to the area in which you feel you **should spend** the most time, ranking all items accordingly until you have marked a "9" next to the area in which you feel you should spend the least time.

A.

DO Spend Time	Area of Responsibility	SHOULD Spend Time
_____	(01) *Program Development* (curriculum, instructional leadership, etc.)	_____
_____	(02) *Personnel* (evaluating, advising, conferring, recruiting, etc.)	_____
_____	(03) *Management* (weekly calendar, office, budget, memos, etc.)	_____
_____	(04) *Student Activities* (meetings, supervision, planning, etc.)	_____
_____	(05) *Student Behavior* (discipline, attendance, meetings, etc.)	_____
_____	(06) *Community* (PTA, advisory groups, parent conferences, etc.)	_____
_____	(07) *District Office* (meetings, task forces, reports, etc.)	_____
_____	(08) *Professional Development* (reading, conferences, etc.)	_____
_____	(09) *Planning* (annual, long range)	_____

23. *Duties and Responsibilities of Assistant Principals.* Principals have final responsibility for everything that happens in a school, but assistant principals share in differing degrees in that responsibility. Please indicate the job profile of the assistant principal(s) in your school in the following chart. Please check the "not applicable" box for any function that does not apply.

Directions:

RESPONSIBILITY	IMPORTANCE	DISCRETIONARY BEHAVIOR
In the appropriate column, indicate the **degree of responsibility** assistant principals have for each duty delegated. Circle the number: (01) Slight —The principal does the job. APs may aid at his direction. (02) Shared—Delegated with close supervision; principal and assistant principals work together. (03) Full —Delegated with general supervision; assistant principals are held responsible for the job.	In the appropriate column, indicate the **degree of importance** you believe the **delegated** duty has to the proper functioning of the school. Circle the number: (01) Least importance (02) Minor importance (03) Average importance (04) Major importance (05) Most importance	In the appropriate column, indicate your judgment of the **level of discretionary** behavior involved in the completion of any **delegated** duty in **your** school. (A duty may be of relatively minor importance and yet it could involve high discretionary behavior. The reverse may be equally true.) Circle the number: (01) Low —Behavior that is directed in large measure by others; behavior that involves restricted high order decision making. (02) High —Behavior that is self-directing, involving high order decision making.

	SAMPLE RESPONSES											
	NOT APPLICABLE	Degree of Responsibility			Degree of Importance					Level of Discretionary Behavior		
Illustrated Examples		SLIGHT	SHARED	FULL	LEAST	MINOR	AVERAGE	MAJOR	MOST	LOW		HIGH
Responsibility for:												
01 Faculty Socials	☐	1	2	③	1	②	3	4	5	1		②
02 "Career day" conferences	☐	①	2	3	1	2	3	④	5	①		2
03 Report card procedures	☑	1	2	3	1	2	3	4	5	1		2

	N O T A P P L I C A B L E	Degree of Responsibility			Degree of Importance					Level of Discretionary Behavior	
Circle Appropriate Code Numbers (For an item that is not applicable to your school situation, place a check (✔) in the NA box after the item).		S L I G H T	S H A R E D	F U L L	L E A S T	M I N O R	A V E R A G E	M A J O R	M O S T	L O W	H I G H
Responsibility for:											
Curriculum and Instruction											
(01) Articulation with feeder schools	☐	1	2	3	1	2	3	4	5	1	2
(02) Curriculum development	☐	1	2	3	1	2	3	4	5	1	2
(03) Evaluation of teachers	☐	1	2	3	1	2	3	4	5	1	2
(04) Innovations, experiments, and research	☐	1	2	3	1	2	3	4	5	1	2
(05) Instructional media and materials	☐	1	2	3	1	2	3	4	5	1	2
(06) Instructional methods	☐	1	2	3	1	2	3	4	5	1	2
(07) Instructional software	☐	1	2	3	1	2	3	4	5	1	2
(08) School-wide examinations	☐	1	2	3	1	2	3	4	5	1	2
(09) School master schedule	☐	1	2	3	1	2	3	4	5	1	2
(10) Staff inservice	☐	1	2	3	1	2	3	4	5	1	2
(11) Textbook selection	☐	1	2	3	1	2	3	4	5	1	2
(12) Work-study program	☐	1	2	3	1	2	3	4	5	1	2
Responsibility for:											
Community Relations											
(13) Administrative representative at community functions	☐	1	2	3	1	2	3	4	5	1	2
(14) Adult education program	☐	1	2	3	1	2	3	4	5	1	2
(15) Coordinating community resources for instruction	☐	1	2	3	1	2	3	4	5	1	2
(16) Informing public of school achievements	☐	1	2	3	1	2	3	4	5	1	2
(17) Liaison with community youth-serving agencies	☐	1	2	3	1	2	3	4	5	1	2
(18) Parent-Teacher Association	☐	1	2	3	1	2	3	4	5	1	2
(19) School alumni association	☐	1	2	3	1	2	3	4	5	1	2
(20) School public relations program	☐	1	2	3	1	2	3	4	5	1	2
(21) School participation in community fund drives	☐	1	2	3	1	2	3	4	5	1	2
Responsibility for:											
School Management											
(22) Building use—nonschool-related	☐	1	2	3	1	2	3	4	5	1	2
(23) Building use—school-related	☐	1	2	3	1	2	3	4	5	1	2
(24) Cafeteria services	☐	1	2	3	1	2	3	4	5	1	2
(25) Clerical services	☐	1	2	3	1	2	3	4	5	1	2
(26) Computer services	☐	1	2	3	1	2	3	4	5	1	2
(27) Custodial services	☐	1	2	3	1	2	3	4	5	1	2

Circle Appropriate Code Numbers (For an item that is not applicable to your school situation, place a check (✔) in the NA box after the item).	NOT APPLICABLE	Degree of Responsibility			Degree of Importance					Level of Discretionary Behavior	
		SLIGHT	SHARED	FULL	LEAST	MINOR	AVERAGE	MAJOR	MOST	LOW	HIGH
(28) Emergency arrangements	☐	1	2	3	1	2	3	4	5	1	2
(29) Graduation activities	☐	1	2	3	1	2	3	4	5	1	2
(30) Noninstructional equipment and supplies	☐	1	2	3	1	2	3	4	5	1	2
(31) School budget	☐	1	2	3	1	2	3	4	5	1	2
(32) School calendars	☐	1	2	3	1	2	3	4	5	1	2
(33) School daily bulletins	☐	1	2	3	1	2	3	4	5	1	2
(34) School financial accounts	☐	1	2	3	1	2	3	4	5	1	2
(35) School policies	☐	1	2	3	1	2	3	4	5	1	2
(36) Special arrangements at start and close of school year	☐	1	2	3	1	2	3	4	5	1	2
(37) Transportation services	☐	1	2	3	1	2	3	4	5	1	2

Responsibility for:

Staff Personnel

Circle Appropriate Code Numbers	NOT APPLICABLE	SLIGHT	SHARED	FULL	LEAST	MINOR	AVERAGE	MAJOR	MOST	LOW	HIGH
(38) Faculty meetings	☐	1	2	3	1	2	3	4	5	1	2
(39) Orientation program for new teachers	☐	1	2	3	1	2	3	4	5	1	2
(40) Student teachers	☐	1	2	3	1	2	3	4	5	1	2
(41) Substitute teachers	☐	1	2	3	1	2	3	4	5	1	2
(42) Teacher "duty" rosters	☐	1	2	3	1	2	3	4	5	1	2
(43) Teacher personnel records	☐	1	2	3	1	2	3	4	5	1	2
(44) Teacher incentives, motivation	☐	1	2	3	1	2	3	4	5	1	2
(45) Teacher selection	☐	1	2	3	1	2	3	4	5	1	2

Responsibility for:

Student Activities

Circle Appropriate Code Numbers	NOT APPLICABLE	SLIGHT	SHARED	FULL	LEAST	MINOR	AVERAGE	MAJOR	MOST	LOW	HIGH
(46) Assemblies	☐	1	2	3	1	2	3	4	5	1	2
(47) Athletic program	☐	1	2	3	1	2	3	4	5	1	2
(48) School club program	☐	1	2	3	1	2	3	4	5	1	2
(49) School dances	☐	1	2	3	1	2	3	4	5	1	2
(50) School newspaper	☐	1	2	3	1	2	3	4	5	1	2
(51) School traffic or safety squad	☐	1	2	3	1	2	3	4	5	1	2
(52) Student council	☐	1	2	3	1	2	3	4	5	1	2
(53) Student photographs	☐	1	2	3	1	2	3	4	5	1	2
(54) Student store	☐	1	2	3	1	2	3	4	5	1	2

Responsibility for:

Student Services

Circle Appropriate Code Numbers	NOT APPLICABLE	SLIGHT	SHARED	FULL	LEAST	MINOR	AVERAGE	MAJOR	MOST	LOW	HIGH
(55) Financial aid for students	☐	1	2	3	1	2	3	4	5	1	2
(56) Guidance program	☐	1	2	3	1	2	3	4	5	1	2
(57) Instruction for home-bound students	☐	1	2	3	1	2	3	4	5	1	2

Circle Appropriate Code Numbers (For an item that is not applicable to your school situation, place a check (✔) in the NA box after the item).	NOT APPLICABLE	Degree of Responsibility			Degree of Importance					Level of Discretionary Behavior	
		SLIGHT	SHARED	FULL	LEAST	MINOR	AVERAGE	MAJOR	MOST	LOW	HIGH
(58) Medical, dental, and health services	☐	1	2	3	1	2	3	4	5	1	2
(59) Orientation program for new students	☐	1	2	3	1	2	3	4	5	1	2
(60) Relationships with educational and employer representatives	☐	1	2	3	1	2	3	4	5	1	2
(61) School assistance to students in transition from school to post-school life	☐	1	2	3	1	2	3	4	5	1	2
(62) Special education (IEPs)	☐	1	2	3	1	2	3	4	5	1	2
(63) Student attendance	☐	1	2	3	1	2	3	4	5	1	2
(64) Student discipline	☐	1	2	3	1	2	3	4	5	1	2
(65) Student testing program	☐	1	2	3	1	2	3	4	5	1	2

24. Please complete the chart below for your school. For each subject area, indicate whether the number of **credit hours** required in grades 9-12 to graduate has stayed the same, decreased, or increased during the past **five years**. In the final column, assess the **impact** of these changes on the various subject areas by checking the **three** in which the impact has been greatest.

Subject	Credit Hours			Impact
	Decreased	Same	Increased	(Check Three)
(01) Agriculture				
(02) Business Education				
(03) Computer Literacy/Skills				
(04) English/Language Arts				
(05) Fine Arts				
(06) Foreign Languages				
(07) Home Economics				
(08) Mathematics				
(09) Physical Education				
(10) Science				
(11) Social Sciences				
(12) Vocational Education				

112

25. What has happened in your school during the past *five years* to the number of credit hours of *electives* that a student may choose to meet *minimum* requirements for graduation?

   (01) Number of elective hours has stayed the same.
   (02) Number of elective hours has increased.
   (03) Number of elective hours has decreased.

26. In the chart below, several practices are listed for making decisions about promotion or graduation. Please check the practices that are actually used in your school and which practices you would prefer.

	Used in Our School		Would Prefer	
	Promotion	Graduation	Promotion	Graduation
(01) Standardized tests—local				
(02) Mastery tests				
(03) Competency tests				
(04) Standardized tests—state				
(05) Comprehensive exit exam				
(06) Minimum grade point average				
(07) Other:				

27. What percentage of your students are *tracked* in the following programs of study? Circle (01) if you have no formal tracking.

   (01) Does not apply
   (02) ____ College-bound; college preparatory
   (03) ____ Vocational-technical
   (04) ____ General

28. What practices are used to assign students to classes or levels of instruction? Do *not* consider students classified as "exceptional" ("gifted and talented," "learning disability," "special needs"). In the chart below, check all the grouping practices that apply to each subject area.

Subjects	Grouping Practice				
	Grade Point Average	Standardized Tests	Student Interest or Choice	Teacher Recommendation	No Special Criteria
(01) Agriculture					
(02) Business Education					
(03) Computer Literacy/Skills					
(04) English/Language Arts					
(05) Fine Arts					
(06) Foreign Languages					
(07) Home Economics					
(08) Mathematics					
(09) Physical Education					
(10) Science					
(11) Social Sciences					
(12) Vocational Education					

29. Does your school have classes of two or more periods in which two or more subjects are combined or correlated (e.g., "core," "general education," "basic skills," "humanities," etc.)?

   (01) Yes   (02) No

113

30. How many hours a week apart from required supervision do you spend informally visiting classrooms or discussing teaching with teachers?

(01) None
(02) 1-3 hours
(03) 4-6 hours

(04) 7-9 hours
(05) 10 or more hours

31. Who has the *most* influence in the selection of instructional content and materials for your school? Check only *one group* for each category.

	Subject Content	Textbooks	Library Books
Teachers			
Principal/School Administrators			
District Supervisors			
School Board			
Parents			
No opinion/Not sure			

32. Does your school have a standing faculty curriculum committee?

(01) Yes

(02) No

33. In which subject areas does a full-time supervisor work with your teachers on a regular basis? *Circle all that apply.*

(01) Agriculture
(02) Business Education
(03) Computer Literacy/Skills
(04) English/Language Arts
(05) Fine Arts (Art, Music, Theatre)
(06) Foreign Languages

(07) Home Economics
(08) Mathematics
(09) Physical Education
(10) Science
(11) Social Sciences
(12) Vocational Education

34. What practices are used for admitting or retaining students in gifted and talented programs (including advanced placement)? *Circle all that apply.*

(01) No programs for gifted and talented.
(02) Selection is based on standardized *achievement* tests.
(03) Selection is based on standardized *aptitude* tests.
(04) Selection is by teacher nomination or recommendation.
(05) Selection is based on prior grade point average.
(06) Selection is by student choice and interest.
(07) Students may be dropped from program based on their grades.
(08) Students may be dropped from program based on standardized achievement test performance.
(09) Students may be dropped from program based on subsequent standardized aptitude test performance.
(10) Other: _____

35. Which of the following organizational formats best describe the gifted and/or talented program in your school? *Circle all appropriate responses.*

(01) No gifted/ talented program
(02) Full-time program
(03) Released time during school hour (special class or "pull-out program")
(04) Regular classes with individualized projects for the gifted/talented
(05) Internship/mentor program
(06) Resource rooms
(07) After school, evening, or weekend program
(08) Summer program
(09) Specialized school in district
(10) Cooperative program with college or university
(11) Program offered in conjunction with district, region, or state department of education
(12) Other: _____

36. Identify the types of programs in which students of your school may enroll. *Circle all that apply.*

    (01) College level courses   (05) Community volunteer programs
    (02) Credit by examination   (06) Summer school enrichment or remediation programs
    (03) Credit by contract or independent study   (07) Other: _____
    (04) Off-campus work experience

37. Estimate the percentage of your students participating this year in community-based programs (e.g., job experience, community services, etc)?

    (01) 0-19%   (03) 40-59%   (05) 80-100%
    (02) 20-39%   (04) 60-79%

38. Is your school accredited by a regional accrediting association?

    (01) Yes   (02) No

39. Rate the quality of administrative articulation of your high school program with elementary/middle and college levels. (Articulation is defined as the coordination of efforts between school levels.) Considering the various alternatives, indicate the status of articulation in the following areas by *checking the appropriate boxes.*

	ELEMENTARY/MIDDLE LEVEL ARTICULATION		COLLEGE ARTICULATION	
	Satisfactory	Unsatisfactory	Satisfactory	Unsatisfactory
(01) Student records				
(02) Student promotion policies				
(03) Granting of subject credit				
(04) Subject content and sequence				
(05) Counseling services				

40. Much has been written about the tasks of American schools. Please rank the 11 statements below according to your belief about their relative importance as educational purposes.

    Assign a rank of "1" to the statement you consider most important, a rank of "2" to the next most important, until you assign a rank of "11" to the statement you consider least important.

_____(01) Acquisition of basic skills (reading, writing, speaking, computing, etc.)
_____(02) Appreciation for and experience with the fine arts
_____(03) Career planning and training in beginning occupational skills
_____(04) Development of moral and spiritual values
_____(05) Development of positive self-concept and good human relations
_____(06) Development of skills and practice in critical intellectual inquiry and problem solving
_____(07) Development of skills to operate in a technological society (engineering, scientific, etc.)
_____(08) Knowledge about and skills in preparation for family life (e.g., sex education, home management, problems of aging, etc.)
_____(09) Preparation for a changing world
_____(10) Physical fitness and useful leisure time sports
_____(11) Understanding of the American value system (its political, economic, social values, etc.)

41. Please indicate your reactions to the following broad educational issues that affect high schools across the country. Check the response after each statement that most closely reflects your view.

	Agree Without Reservation	Agree With Some Reservations	Agree With Many Reservations	Do Not Agree
(01) The principle of *universal* secondary education is essential to American society.				
(02) Federal aid must be made available to private and religious secondary schools.				
(03) Certain limitations should be placed upon classroom discussion of political "isms" and "anti-isms."				
(04) Schools require too little academic work of students. *Note:* Base your response to this item only on your own school.				
(05) Each subject taught in schools should be justifiable as practical.				
(06) Grouping according to IQ or achievement scores is desirable in academic subjects such as math, English, and foreign languages.				
(07) The academic year (compulsory) should be lengthened.				
(08) Youths who are disinterested or hostile toward schooling should *not* be required to attend.				
(09) School attendance should be compulsory until high school graduation or age 18.				
(10) Schools should provide a general intellectual background and leave specific job training to other agencies.				
(11) Schools should implement proven diagnostic-prescriptive strategies to personalize learning for all students.				
(12) Schools should develop special programs for educating academically talented students.				
(13) Schools should design special programs for the handicapped, ethnic minorities, and non-English-speaking.				
(14) School programs should include specific instruction on alcohol and drug abuse.				
(15) Specific criteria, based on teaching effectiveness research, should be regularly employed in teacher evaluation.				
(16) Various teacher incentives such as differential pay and career ladders should be implemented in place of salary schedules and fixed assignments.				
(17) More stringent requirements are needed for all students in the traditional academic subjects.				
(18) Standardized testing of students in all subjects is necessary to improve instruction.				
(19) Functional computer competence is essential for all students.				

42. All things considered (learning conditions, teaching staff, capital outlay, etc.), what is your judgment about the optimum number of students in a high school? In deciding, focus on the current school year.

(01) Fewer than 500
(02) 500-599
(03) 600-999
(04) 1,000-1,499
(05) 1,500-1,999
(06) 2,000-2,499
(07) 2,500-2,999
(08) 3,000 or more

116

43. In your opinion, if school classes are maintained at about their present size, do technological advances such as interactive videodisc instruction and computer-assisted education hold real promise for improving teaching and learning in schools?

    (01) Yes, considerable promise   (04) No, would be definitely harmful
    (02) Yes, some promise   (05) No opinion
    (03) No, little if any promise

44. Would you be in favor of some system of individualized promotion for students rather than the customary grade placement and promotion?

    (01) Yes   (04) No
    (02) Yes, we have such a system   (05) No opinion
    (03) Some advantages, some disadvantages

45. Are you in favor of some rigorous check of attainment of basic skills (e.g., competency testing)?

    (01) Yes   (04) No
    (02) Yes, we have such a system   (05) No opinion
    (03) Some advantages, some disadvantages

46. Do you favor the idea of a "multiple-diploma" or "diploma and certificate" plan for students who have failed to achieve a minimum mastery of certain basic subjects?

    (01) Yes   (04) No
    (02) Yes, we have such a system   (05) No opinion
    (03) Some advantages, some disadvantages

47. What should be required for certification of principals? *Circle any item you think should be a requirement.*

    (01) A teaching certificate
    (02) A Master's degree
    (03) A specified number of years of teaching experience
    (04) A graduate degree beyond the Master's degree
    (05) Specific courses in school administration
    (06) Specific courses in professional education other than school administration
    (07) Specific courses in curriculum development and instructional leadership
    (08) An internship or other professional field experiences
    (09) A professional examination to test knowledge of administration
    (10) Assessment of behaviors and skills (e.g., through practices such as NASSP's Assessment Center)
    (11) Monitoring after placement by professional observers to maintain certification
    (12) No requirements

48. Should principals have tenure as administrators?

    (01) Yes   (02) No

In your opinion, which of the statements in the following three questions best characterize the role of the principal? *Circle only one answer for each question.*

49. Choose *one*

    (01) The principal primarily should represent the interests of parents, leaders, and patrons of the school.
    (02) The principal should take initiative in developing and implementing school policy according to his/her best professional judgment.

50. Choose *one*

    (01) The principal should effectively and efficiently manage the day-to-day affairs of the school.
    (02) The principal should lead the school in new educational directions according to his/her best professional judgment.

51. Choose *one*

   (01) The principal should play the major role in establishing the agenda and deciding the important issues in the school.
   (02) The principal should share decision making with the faculty on important school issues.

52. Below is a list of conditions or developments which many believe have a general influence upon secondary education. Please indicate how you feel each will influence *your* school during the *next three to five years.*

   Check the appropriate space to indicate whether the condition or development will have (1) no influence, (2) some influence, or (3) strong influence on your school.

Condition	No Influence	Some Influence	Strong Influence
(01) Accountability movement			
(02) Alcohol abuse			
(03) Attention to academic achievement			
(04) Change in government funding			
(05) Changing family structure			
(06) Child abuse (physical, sexual)			
(07) Community participation			
(08) Community-based learning			
(09) Competency testing of students			
(10) Demand for basics			
(11) Drug abuse			
(12) Enrollment decline			
(13) Enrollment increase			
(14) Finance and general economy			
(15) Graduation requirements			
(16) New technologies			
(17) Personalized/effective education movement			
(18) Student attendance problems			
(19) Student motivation			
(20) Teacher competency			
(21) Teacher incentives			
(22) Teacher motivation			
(23) Teacher shortage			
(24) Teen emotional/psychological problems (runaways, suicide, etc.)			
(25) Teen sexual activity			
(26) Youth gang activity			
(27) Youth unemployment			
(28) Other: _____			

NATIONAL ASSOCIATION OF SECONDARY SCHOOL PRINCIPALS

Reston, Virginia 22091

A National Study of High School Leaders and Their Schools

SURVEY OF ASSISTANT PRINCIPALS

Form A

DIRECTIONS

Your questionnaire is identified by the label placed on it. It is not necessary to sign or place your name on the questionnaire. In reporting results, only statistical summaries of the responses of groups of assistant principals will be cited. In no case will the identity of an individual be divulged. You are urged to make every answer a sincere one.

Circle the number of the appropriate response using pen or pencil. If you change a response, please make the change distinctly so there is no doubt about how you wish to answer.

Attempt to answer every question. For some questions none of the alternatives may correspond exactly to your situation or to the opinion you hold. In such cases mark the alternative that comes closest to the answer you would like to give.

This study is being conducted to investigate the duties and responsibilities assigned to Assistant, Vice, and/or Associate Principals. Previous studies indicate that the duties and responsibilities of this position may vary from school to school.

> We would like to know what YOUR operating practices are and what is expected of YOU in your school.

Place your completed questionnaire in the envelope provided and mail it to NASSP. Thank you for your cooperation and assistance in this important study.

••

Advisory Committee for A Study of High School Leaders and Their Schools:

Patricia D. Campbell, Lakewood High School, Lakewood, Colorado; Glen M. DeHaven, Oldtown School, Oldtown, Maryland; Richard Gorton, School of Education, University of Wisconsin–Milwaukee; Jacqueline H. Simmons, Paul Robeson High School, Chicago, Illinois; Norman O. Stevens, Mill River Union High School, North Clarendon, Vermont; Michael K. Thomas, Vashon High School, St. Louis, Missouri; Peggy Walters, J. Frank Dobie High School, Houston, Texas; Gary P. Wells, Henley High School, Klamath Falls, Oregon; Jeannette Wheatley, Cass Technical High School, Detroit, Michigan; James V. Wright, Fremont Ross High School, Fremont, Ohio.

Research Team:

Lorin W. Anderson, University of South Carolina; Edgar A. Kelley, Western Michigan University; Lloyd E. McCleary, University of Utah; Leonard O. Pellicer, University of South Carolina; James W. Keefe, NASSP

1. What is your sex?　　　　(01) Male　　　　(02) Female

2. What is your age?

   (01) 23 or under　　　　(04) 35-39　　　　(07) 50-54
   (02) 24-29　　　　　　　(05) 40-44　　　　(08) 55-59
   (03) 30-34　　　　　　　(06) 45-49　　　　(09) 60 or older

3. With which ethnic group would you identify yourself?

   (01) White　　　　　(03) Hispanic　　　　　(05) Asian
   (02) Black　　　　　(04) American Indian　　(06) Other: _____

4. In which of the following areas did you major as an ***undergraduate? Select only one answer.***

   (01) Secondary education (other than physical education)
   (02) Physical education
   (03) Elementary education
   (04) Humanities (literature, languages, etc.)
   (05) Physical or biological sciences
   (06) Social sciences (sociology, history, etc.)
   (07) Mathematics
   (08) Fine arts
   (09) Business
   (10) Vocational-Technical (home economics, industrial arts, etc.)
   (11) Other: _____

5. What is the highest degree you have earned?

   (01) Less than a BA
   (02) Bachelor's Degree
   (03) Master's Degree in Education
   (04) Master's Degree not in Education
   (05) Master's Degree plus some additional graduate work
   (06) Educational Specialist, six-year program or equivalent
   (07) Master's Degree plus ***all course work*** for a doctorate
   (08) Doctor of Education
   (09) Doctor of Philosophy
   (10) Other: _____

6. At what age did you enter teaching? _____

7. How many years of ***teaching*** experience, regardless of level, did you have prior to taking your present position? Do not include years as a full-time administrator, supervisor, counselor, psychologist, or librarian.

   (01) None　　　　　(04) 4-6 years　　　　(07) 15-19 years
   (02) One year　　　(05) 7-9 years　　　　(08) 20-24 years
   (03) 2-3 years　　　(06) 10-14 years　　　(09) 25 or more years

8. At what age did you enter educational administration? _____

9. At what career point did you decide to enter educational administration?

   (01) About the same time I decided to enter the educational profession.
   (02) After my first few years in the profession.
   (03) After considerable experience (5 years or more).

10. What was the last position you held prior to becoming a high school assistant principal? *Select only one answer.*

(01) Teacher
(02) Assistant principal of an elementary or middle level school
(03) Assistant principal of another high school
(04) Principal of an elementary or middle level school
(05) Guidance counselor
(06) Other—education, specify: _____
(07) Other—non-education, specify: _____

11. How many years did you serve in your last position before becoming a high school assistant principal?

(01) One year   (03) 4-5 years   (05) 8-9 years
(02) 2-3 years   (04) 6-7 years   (06) 10 or more years

12. What is your official job title?

(01) Assistant principal   (03) Associate principal
(02) Vice principal   (04) Other: _____

13. At what age were you appointed to your first assistant principalship?

(01) 23 or under   (04) 35-39   (07) 50-54
(02) 24-29   (05) 40-44   (08) 55-59
(03) 30-34   (06) 45-49   (09) 60 or older

14. How many years have you served as an assistant principal, including this school year?

(01) One year   (04) 6-7 years   (07) 15-19 years
(02) 2-3 years   (05) 8-9 years   (08) 20-24 years
(03) 4-5 years   (06) 10-14 years   (09) 25 or more years

15. How long have you been an assistant principal in this school, including this school year?

(01) One year   (04) 4-5 years   (07) 12-14 years
(02) Two years   (05) 6-8 years   (08) 15-17 years
(03) Three years   (06) 9-11 years   (09) 18 or more years

16. Which of the following categories best describes the high school in which you serve as assistant principal? *Choose only one answer.*

(01) Public comprehensive   (05) Private, religious affiliated
(02) Public "alternative"   (06) Private, not religious affiliated
(03) Public special (commercial, vocational, arts, etc.)   (07) Other, specify _____
(04) Parochial or diocesan

17. What grades are included in your school?

(01) Kindergarten-12   (05) 9-12
(02) 1-12   (06) 10-12
(03) 7-12   (07) 11-12
(04) 8-12   (08) Other, specify _____

18. How many high school students (grade 9 and above) were enrolled in your school on October 1st of the current school year?

(01) Fewer than 250   (04) 750-999   (07) 2,000-2,499
(02) 250-499   (05) 1,000-1,499   (08) 2,500 or more
(03) 500-749   (06) 1,500-1,999

19. In which geographic region is your school located?

(01) New England   (04) Midwest   (07) West Coast
(02) Mid-Atlantic   (05) Southwest   (08) Non-contiguous
(03) South   (06) Inter Mountain   (09) Other, specify _____

20. Which of the following population categories best describes the locale of the high school of which you are assistant principal?

(01) City, more than 1,000,000
(02) City, 150,000-999,999
(03) Suburban, related to city of 150,000 or more

(04) City, 25,000-149,999, distinct from a metropolitan area
(05) City, 5,000-24,999, not suburban
(06) Town or rural under 5,000

21. What is your current annual salary as assistant principal? Do not include fringe benefits.

(01) Less than $20,000
(02) 20,000-24,999
(03) 25,000-29,999

(04) 30,000-34,999
(05) 35,000-39,999
(06) 40,000-44,999

(07) 45,000-49,999
(08) 50,000-54,999
(09) 55,000 or more
(10) Not applicable (religious order)

22. **Duties and Responsibilities of Assistant Principals.** Principals have final responsibility for everything that happens in a school, but assistant principals share in differing degrees in that responsibility. Please indicate the job profile of the assistant principal(s) in your school in the following chart. Please check the "not applicable" box for any function that does not apply.

Directions:

RESPONSIBILITY	IMPORTANCE	DISCRETIONARY BEHAVIOR
In the appropriate column, indicate the **degree of responsibility** assistant principals have for each duty delegated. Circle the number: (01) Slight —The principal does the job. APs may aid at his direction. (02) Shared—Delegated with close supervision; principal and assistant principals work together. (03) Full —Delegated with general supervision; assistant principals are held responsible for the job.	In the appropriate column, indicate the **degree of importance** you believe the **delegated** duty has to the proper functioning of the school. Circle the number: (01) Least importance (02) Minor importance (03) Average importance (04) Major importance (05) Most importance	In the appropriate column, indicate your judgment of the **level of discretionary** behavior involved in the completion of any **delegated** duty in **your** school. (A duty may be of relatively minor importance and yet it could involve high discretionary behavior. The reverse may be equally true.) Circle the number: (01) Low —Behavior that is directed in large measure by others; behavior that involves restricted high order decision making. (02) High —Behavior that is self-directing, involving high order decision making.

	SAMPLE RESPONSES									
	NOT APPLICABLE	Degree of Responsibility			Degree of Importance					Level of Discretionary Behavior	
Illustrated Examples		SLIGHT	SHARED	FULL	LEAST	MINOR	AVERAGE	MAJOR	MOST	LOW	HIGH
Responsibility for:											
01 Faculty Socials	☐	1	2	③	1	②	3	4	5	1	②
02 "Career day" conferences	☐	①	2	3	1	2	3	④	5	①	2
03 Report card procedures	☑	1	2	3	1	2	3	4	5	1	2

Circle Appropriate Code Numbers (For an item that is not applicable to your school situation, place a check (✔) in the NA box after the item).	NOT APPLICABLE	Degree of Responsibility			Degree of Importance					Level of Discretionary Behavior	
		SLIGHT	SHARED	FULL	LEAST	MINOR	AVERAGE	MAJOR	MOST	LOW	HIGH
Responsibility for:											
Curriculum and Instruction											
(01) Articulation with feeder schools	☐	1	2	3	1	2	3	4	5	1	2
(02) Curriculum development	☐	1	2	3	1	2	3	4	5	1	2
(03) Evaluation of teachers	☐	1	2	3	1	2	3	4	5	1	2
(04) Innovations, experiments, and research	☐	1	2	3	1	2	3	4	5	1	2
(05) Instructional media and materials	☐	1	2	3	1	2	3	4	5	1	2
(06) Instructional methods	☐	1	2	3	1	2	3	4	5	1	2
(07) Instructional software	☐	1	2	3	1	2	3	4	5	1	2
(08) School-wide examinations	☐	1	2	3	1	2	3	4	5	1	2
(09) School master schedule	☐	1	2	3	1	2	3	4	5	1	2
(10) Staff inservice	☐	1	2	3	1	2	3	4	5	1	2
(11) Textbook selection	☐	1	2	3	1	2	3	4	5	1	2
(12) Work-study program	☐	1	2	3	1	2	3	4	5	1	2
Responsibility for:											
Community Relations											
(13) Administrative representative at community functions	☐	1	2	3	1	2	3	4	5	1	2
(14) Adult education program	☐	1	2	3	1	2	3	4	5	1	2
(15) Coordinating community resources for instruction	☐	1	2	3	1	2	3	4	5	1	2
(16) Informing public of school achievements	☐	1	2	3	1	2	3	4	5	1	2
(17) Liaison with community youth-serving agencies	☐	1	2	3	1	2	3	4	5	1	2
(18) Parent-Teacher Association	☐	1	2	3	1	2	3	4	5	1	2
(19) School alumni association	☐	1	2	3	1	2	3	4	5	1	2
(20) School public relations program	☐	1	2	3	1	2	3	4	5	1	2
(21) School participation in community fund drives	☐	1	2	3	1	2	3	4	5	1	2
Responsibility for:											
School Management											
(22) Building use—nonschool-related	☐	1	2	3	1	2	3	4	5	1	2
(23) Building use—school-related	☐	1	2	3	1	2	3	4	5	1	2
(24) Cafeteria services	☐	1	2	3	1	2	3	4	5	1	2
(25) Clerical services	☐	1	2	3	1	2	3	4	5	1	2
(26) Computer services	☐	1	2	3	1	2	3	4	5	1	2
(27) Custodial services	☐	1	2	3	1	2	3	4	5	1	2

	NOT APPLICABLE	Degree of Responsibility			Degree of Importance					Level of Discretionary Behavior	
Circle Appropriate Code Numbers (For an item that is not applicable to your school situation, place a check (✔) in the NA box after the item).		SLIGHT	SHARED	FULL	LEAST	MINOR	AVERAGE	MAJOR	MOST	LOW	HIGH
(28) Emergency arrangements	☐	1	2	3	1	2	3	4	5	1	2
(29) Graduation activities	☐	1	2	3	1	2	3	4	5	1	2
(30) Noninstructional equipment and supplies	☐	1	2	3	1	2	3	4	5	1	2
(31) School budget	☐	1	2	3	1	2	3	4	5	1	2
(32) School calendars	☐	1	2	3	1	2	3	4	5	1	2
(33) School daily bulletins	☐	1	2	3	1	2	3	4	5	1	2
(34) School financial accounts	☐	1	2	3	1	2	3	4	5	1	2
(35) School policies	☐	1	2	3	1	2	3	4	5	1	2
(36) Special arrangements at start and close of school year	☐	1	2	3	1	2	3	4	5	1	2
(37) Transportation services	☐	1	2	3	1	2	3	4	5	1	2

Responsibility for:

Staff Personnel

	NOT APPLICABLE	SLIGHT	SHARED	FULL	LEAST	MINOR	AVERAGE	MAJOR	MOST	LOW	HIGH
(38) Faculty meetings	☐	1	2	3	1	2	3	4	5	1	2
(39) Orientation program for new teachers	☐	1	2	3	1	2	3	4	5	1	2
(40) Student teachers	☐	1	2	3	1	2	3	4	5	1	2
(41) Substitute teachers	☐	1	2	3	1	2	3	4	5	1	2
(42) Teacher "duty" rosters	☐	1	2	3	1	2	3	4	5	1	2
(43) Teacher personnel records	☐	1	2	3	1	2	3	4	5	1	2
(44) Teacher incentives, motivation	☐	1	2	3	1	2	3	4	5	1	2
(45) Teacher selection	☐	1	2	3	1	2	3	4	5	1	2

Responsibility for:

Student Activities

	NOT APPLICABLE	SLIGHT	SHARED	FULL	LEAST	MINOR	AVERAGE	MAJOR	MOST	LOW	HIGH
(46) Assemblies	☐	1	2	3	1	2	3	4	5	1	2
(47) Athletic program	☐	1	2	3	1	2	3	4	5	1	2
(48) School club program	☐	1	2	3	1	2	3	4	5	1	2
(49) School dances	☐	1	2	3	1	2	3	4	5	1	2
(50) School newspaper	☐	1	2	3	1	2	3	4	5	1	2
(51) School traffic or safety squad	☐	1	2	3	1	2	3	4	5	1	2
(52) Student council	☐	1	2	3	1	2	3	4	5	1	2
(53) Student photographs	☐	1	2	3	1	2	3	4	5	1	2
(54) Student store	☐	1	2	3	1	2	3	4	5	1	2

Responsibility for:

Student Services

	NOT APPLICABLE	SLIGHT	SHARED	FULL	LEAST	MINOR	AVERAGE	MAJOR	MOST	LOW	HIGH
(55) Financial aid for students	☐	1	2	3	1	2	3	4	5	1	2
(56) Guidance program	☐	1	2	3	1	2	3	4	5	1	2
(57) Instruction for home-bound students	☐	1	2	3	1	2	3	4	5	1	2

Circle Appropriate Code Numbers (For an item that is not applicable to your school situation, place a check (✓) in the NA box after the item).	NOT APPLICABLE	Degree of Responsibility			Degree of Importance					Level of Discretionary Behavior	
		SLIGHT	SHARED	FULL	LEAST	MINOR	AVERAGE	MAJOR	MOST	LOW	HIGH
(58) Medical, dental, and health services	☐	1	2	3	1	2	3	4	5	1	2
(59) Orientation program for new students	☐	1	2	3	1	2	3	4	5	1	2
(60) Relationships with educational and employer representatives	☐	1	2	3	1	2	3	4	5	1	2
(61) School assistance to students in transition from school to post-school life	☐	1	2	3	1	2	3	4	5	1	2
(62) Special education (IEPs)	☐	1	2	3	1	2	3	4	5	1	2
(63) Student attendance	☐	1	2	3	1	2	3	4	5	1	2
(64) Student discipline	☐	1	2	3	1	2	3	4	5	1	2
(65) Student testing program	☐	1	2	3	1	2	3	4	5	1	2

23. Circle the practice which **best** describes how your salary is determined.

(01) By the board, without consultation or negotiation.
(02) By the board, based upon superintendent's recommendation, without consultation or negotiation.
(03) By the superintendent, without consultation or negotiation.
(04) Through informal and individual negotiations with the board.
(05) Through informal and individual negotiations with the superintendent.
(06) Through informal negotiations with the board as a member of a group of administrators.
(07) Through informal negotiations with the superintendent as a member of a group of administrators.
(08) As a member of a formal bargaining group.
(09) Other: _____

24. Regardless of schedule of payment, what is your yearly salary contract based upon?

(01) 9 or 9½ months
(02) 10 or 10½ months
(03) 11 or 11½ months
(04) 12 months

25. Is your contract a multi-year contract?

(01) No.
(02) Yes—Two year contract.
(03) Yes—Three year contract.
(04) Yes—More than a three year contract.

26. In addition to your salary, which of the following fringe benefits do you receive from your school or district? **Circle all appropriate responses.**

(01) No fringe benefits
(02) Automobile or mileage allowance
(03) College/University tuition for yourself
(04) Dental insurance
(05) Expense account
(06) Housing or equivalent subsidy
(07) Life insurance
(08) Meals
(09) Medical insurance
(10) Retirement
(11) Tuition for dependents (nonpublic school)

27. Do you have tenure **as assistant principal?**   (01) Yes   (02) No

28. On the average, how many hours a week do you work at your job as assistant principal?

(01) Less than 40   (03) 45-49   (05) 55-59
(02) 40-44   (04) 50-54   (06) 60 or more

For the next five questions, circle the number on line A which describes your perception of how your job **actually is;** circle the number on line B to describe how you think your job **should be.**

29. A. How much prestige do you feel your position as assistant principal **provides** you in the community where your school is located?

1	2	3	4	5
Little		Moderate		Much

B. How much prestige do you feel your position as assistant principal **should** provide you in the community where your school is located?

1	2	3	4	5
Little		Moderate		Much

30. A. How much opportunity for independent thought and action **does** your position as assistant principal provide?

1	2	3	4	5
Little		Moderate		Much

B. How much opportunity for independent thought and action **should** your position as assistant principal provide?

1	2	3	4	5
Little		Moderate		Much

31. A. How much self-fulfillment (i.e., the feeling of being able to use one's unique capabilities or realizing one's potential) **does** your position as assistant principal provide?

1	2	3	4	5
Little		Moderate		Much

B. How much self-fulfillment **should** your position as assistant principal provide?

1	2	3	4	5
Little		Moderate		Much

126

32. A. How much job security do you feel you *have* as assistant principal?

1	2	3	4	5
Little		Moderate		Much

B. How much job security do you feel you *should* have as assistant principal?

1	2	3	4	5
Little		Moderate		Much

33. A. How much opportunity to be helpful to other people *does* your position as assistant principal provide?

1	2	3	4	5
Little		Moderate		Much

B. How much opportunity to be helpful to other people *should* your position as assistant principal provide?

1	2	3	4	5
Little		Moderate		Much

34. In how many civic and political organizations (Chamber of Commerce, Rotary, etc.) do you hold active membership?

(01) None   (03) Two   (05) Four
(02) One   (04) Three   (06) Five

35. In how many professional educational organizations do you hold active membership at the state or national level? (Count an organization and its affiliates, such as NASSP and its state affiliates, only once).

(01) NASSP and its affiliates.
(02) NASSP and one other professional education organization.
(03) NASSP and two other professional education organizations.
(04) NASSP and three other professional education organizations.
(05) Other organizations but not NASSP and affiliates.

36. Circle each type of professional development activity in which you have been involved during the last two years.

(01) National professional organization institute or conference (voluntary participation).
(02) State professional organization activity (voluntary participation).
(03) Activity conducted by private consultants at an out-of-district location (voluntary participation).
(04) District activity required as part of employment.
(05) Other district activities (voluntary participation).
(06) Enrollment in graduate courses at an institution of higher education.
(07) State department of education or county agency activity (voluntary participation).
(08) State department of education or county agency activity (required participation).
(09) Principal Center or Academy (voluntary participation).
(10) Other, specify: _____

37. Circle all of the following that apply to your district's support for your participation in the activities of professional educational organizations.

My district:

(01) Discourages active participation in professional organizations.
(02) Encourages active participation at my personal expense.
(03) Pays my membership dues.
(04) Allows released time to attend meetings/conferences.
(05) Pays all or most of my expenses to attend meetings/conferences.
(06) Pays a portion (half or less) of my expenses to attend meetings/conferences.

127

38. Do you teach any regularly scheduled classes?

(01) No   (02) Yes—one course   (03) Yes, two or three courses

39. How many assistant principals are there in your school?

(01) One, part time   (03) Two   (05) None, but I hold an equivalent position
(02) One, full time   (04) Three or more

40. How many female assistant principals are there in your school (including yourself if applicable)?

(01) One   (02) Two   (03) Three or more   (04) None

41. Who assigns the duties and responsibilities of assistant principals in your school?

(01) Principal alone
(02) Superintendent alone
(03) School board alone
(04) Principal in conference with assistant principal
(05) Principal in conference with superintendent and assistant principal
(06) Principal in conference with superintendent, school board, and assistant principal
(07) Principal and superintendent
(08) Principal and school board
(09) Principal in conference with superintendent and school board
(10) Superintendent and school board
(11) Other, please specify _____

42. How important to you were the following statements about jobs and careers at the time that you decided to: A. Enter teaching. B. Enter administration? Please check the most appropriate responses under both A and B for each item below.

Teaching or Administration will:	A. Teaching				B. Assistant Principalship			
	Most Important*	Highly Important	Moderate Importance	Little or No Importance	Most Important*	Highly Important	Moderate Importance	Little or No Importance
(01) Provide me with a chance to make a good salary								
(02) Provide an opportunity to use my special abilities and aptitudes								
(03) Give me social status and prestige								
(04) Give me an opportunity to work with people rather than things								
(05) Permit me to be creative and original								
(06) Give me a chance to exercise leadership								
(07) Enable me to look forward to a stable, secure future								
(08) Give me an opportunity to be helpful to others								
(09) Offer excellent hours and vacations								
(10) Provide an opportunity to work with students								
(11) Offer recognition by superiors								
(12) Give opportunity to improve curriculum and instruction								
(13) Others, please specify: _____ _____								

*May be selected more than once.

43. In which of the following positions have you had one full year or more of experience? *Circle all responses that are appropriate.*

   (01) Athletic coach
   (02) Athletic director
   (03) Counselor or other guidance position
   (04) Dean or registrar
   (05) Department or area chairperson

44. Please indicate your reactions to the following broad educational issues that affect high schools across the country. Check the response after each statement which most closely reflects your view.

	Agree Without Reservation	Agree With Some Reservations	Agree With Many Reservations	Do Not Agree
(01) The principle of *universal* secondary education is essential to American society.				
(02) Federal aid must be made available to private and religious secondary schools.				
(03) Certain limitations should be placed upon classroom discussion of political "isms" and "anti-isms."				
(04) Schools require too little academic work of students. *Note:* Base your response to this item only on your own school.				
(05) Each subject taught in schools should be justifiable as practical.				
(06) Grouping according to IQ or achievement scores is desirable in academic subjects such as math, English, and foreign languages.				
(07) The academic year (compulsory) should be lengthened.				
(08) Youths who are disinterested or hostile toward schooling should not be required to attend.				
(09) School attendance should be compulsory until high school graduation or age 18.				
(10) Schools should provide a general intellectual background and leave specific job training to other agencies.				
(11) Schools should implement proven diagnostic-prescriptive strategies to personalize learning for all students.				
(12) Schools should develop special programs for educating academically talented students.				
(13) Schools should design special programs for the handicapped, ethnic minorities, and non-English-speaking.				
(14) School programs should include specific instruction on alcohol and drug abuse.				
(15) Specific criteria, based on teaching effectiveness research, should be regularly employed in teacher evaluation.				
(16) Various teacher incentives such as differential pay and career ladders should be implemented in place of salary schedules and fixed assignments.				
(17) More stringent requirements are needed for all students in the traditional academic subjects.				
(18) Standardized testing of students in all subjects is necessary to improve instruction.				
(19) Functional computer competence is essential for all students.				

NATIONAL ASSOCIATION OF SECONDARY SCHOOL PRINCIPALS

Reston, Virginia 22091

A National Study of High School Leaders and Their Schools
SURVEY OF ASSISTANT PRINCIPALS

Form B

DIRECTIONS

Your questionnaire is identified by the label placed on it. It is not necessary to sign or place your name on the questionnaire. In reporting results, only statistical summaries of the responses of groups of assistant principals will be cited. In no case will the identity of an individual be divulged. You are urged to make every answer a sincere one.

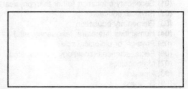

Circle the number of the appropriate response using pen or pencil. If you change a response, please make the change distinctly so there is no doubt about how you wish to answer.

Attempt to answer every question. For some questions none of the alternatives may correspond exactly to your situation or to the opinion you hold. In such cases mark the alternative which comes closest to the answer you would like to give.

This study is being conducted to investigate the duties and responsibilities assigned to Assistant, Vice, and/or Associate Principals. Previous studies indicate that the duties and responsibilities of this position may vary from school to school.

> We would like to know what YOUR operating practices are and what is expected of YOU in your school.

Place your completed questionnaire in the envelope provided and mail it to NASSP. Thank you for your cooperation and assistance in this important study.

••

Advisory Committee for A Study of High School Leaders and Their Schools:

Patricia D. Campbell, Lakewood High School, Lakewood, Colorado; Glen M. DeHaven, Oldtown School, Oldtown, Maryland; Richard Gorton, School of Education, University of Wisconsin–Milwaukee; Jacqueline H. Simmons, Paul Robeson High School, Chicago, Illinois; Norman O. Stevens, Mill River Union High School, North Clarendon, Vermont; Michael K. Thomas, Vashon High School, St. Louis, Missouri; Peggy Walters, J. Frank Dobie High School, Houston, Texas; Gary P. Wells, Henley High School, Klamath Falls, Oregon; Jeannette Wheatley, Cass Technical High School, Detroit, Michigan; James V. Wright, Fremont Ross High School, Fremont, Ohio.

Research Team:

Lorin W. Anderson, University of South Carolina; Edgar A. Kelley, Western Michigan University; Lloyd E. McCleary, University of Utah; Leonard O. Pellicer, University of South Carolina; James W. Keefe, NASSP

131

1. What is your sex?   (01) Male   (02) Female

2. What is your age?

(01) 23 or under   (04) 35-39   (07) 50-54
(02) 24-29   (05) 40-44   (08) 55-59
(03) 30-34   (06) 45-49   (09) 60 or older

3. With which ethnic group would you identify yourself?

(01) White   (03) Hispanic   (05) Asian
(02) Black   (04) American Indian   (06) Other: _____

4. In which of the following areas did you major as an *undergraduate? Select only one answer.*

(01) Secondary education (other than physical education)
(02) Physical education
(03) Elementary education
(04) Humanities (literature, languages, etc.)
(05) Physical or biological sciences
(06) Social sciences (sociology, history, etc.)
(07) Mathematics
(08) Fine arts
(09) Business
(10) Vocational-Technical (home economics, industrial arts, etc.)
(11) Other: _____

5. What is the highest degree you have earned?

(01) Less than a BA
(02) Bachelor's Degree
(03) Master's Degree in Education
(04) Master's Degree not in Education
(05) Master's Degree plus some additional graduate work
(06) Educational Specialist, six-year program or equivalent
(07) Master's Degree plus *all course work* for a doctorate
(08) Doctor of Education
(09) Doctor of Philosophy
(10) Other: _____

6. At what age did you enter teaching? _____

7. How many years of *teaching* experience, regardless of level, did you have prior to taking your present position? Do not include years as a full-time administrator, supervisor, counselor, psychologist, or librarian.

(01) None   (04) 4-6 years   (07) 15-19 years
(02) One year   (05) 7-9 years   (08) 20-24 years
(03) 2-3 years   (06) 10-14 years   (09) 25 or more years

8. At what age did you enter educational administration? _____

9. At what career point did you decide to enter educational administration? _____

(01) About the same time I decided to enter the educational profession.
(02) After my first few years in the profession.
(03) After considerable experience (5 years or more).

10. What was the last position you held prior to becoming a high school assistant principal? *Select only one answer.*

(01) Teacher
(02) Assistant principal of an elementary or middle level school
(03) Assistant principal of another high school
(04) Principal of an elementary or middle level school
(05) Guidance counselor
(06) Other—education, specify: _____
(07) Other—non-education, specify: _____

11. How many years did you serve in your last position before becoming a high school assistant principal?

(01) One year   (03) 4-5 years   (05) 8-9 years
(02) 2-3 years   (04) 6-7 years   (06) 10 or more years

12. What is your official job title?

(01) Assistant principal   (03) Associate principal
(02) Vice principal   (04) Other: _____

13. At what age were you appointed to your first assistant principalship?

(01) 23 or under   (04) 35-39   (07) 50-54
(02) 24-29   (05) 40-44   (08) 55-59
(03) 30-34   (06) 45-49   (09) 60 or older

14. How many years have you served as an assistant principal, including this school year?

(01) One year   (04) 6-7 years   (07) 15-19 years
(02) 2-3 years   (05) 8-9 years   (08) 20-24 years
(03) 4-5 years   (06) 10-14 years   (09) 25 or more years

15. How long have you been an assistant principal in this school, including this school year?

(01) One year   (04) 4-5 years   (07) 12-14 years
(02) Two years   (05) 6-8 years   (08) 15-17 years
(03) Three years   (06) 9-11 years   (09) 18 or more years

16. Which of the following categories best describes the high school in which you serve as assistant principal? *Choose only one answer.*

(01) Public comprehensive   (05) Private, religious affiliated
(02) Public "alternative"   (06) Private, not religious affiliated
(03) Public special (commercial, vocational, arts, etc.)   (07) Other, specify _____
(04) Parochial or diocesan

17. What grades are included in your school?

(01) Kindergarten-12   (05) 9-12
(02) 1-12   (06) 10-12
(03) 7-12   (07) 11-12
(04) 8-12   (08) Other, specify _____

18. How many high school students (grade 9 and above) were enrolled in your school on October 1st of the current school year?

(01) Fewer than 250   (04) 750-999   (07) 2,000-2,499
(02) 250-499   (05) 1,000-1,499   (08) 2,500 or more
(03) 500-749   (06) 1,500-1,999

19. In which geographic region is your school located?

(01) New England   (04) Midwest   (07) West Coast
(02) Mid-Atlantic   (05) Southwest   (08) Non-contiguous
(03) South   (06) Inter Mountain (09) Other, specify _____

20. Which of the following population categories best describes the locale of the high school of which you are assistant principal?

(01) City, more than 1,000,000
(02) City, 150,000-999,999
(03) Suburban, related to city of 150,000 or more

(04) City, 25,000-149,999, distinct from a metropolitan area
(05) City, 5,000-24,999, not suburban
(06) Town or rural under 5,000

21. What is your current annual salary as assistant principal? Do not include fringe benefits.

(01) Less than $20,000
(02) 20,000-24,999
(03) 25,000-29,999

(04) 30,000-34,999
(05) 35,000-39,999
(06) 40,000-44,999

(07) 45,000-49,999
(08) 50,000-54,999
(09) 55,000 or more
(10) Not applicable (religious order)

22. **Duties and Responsibilities of Assistant Principals.** Principals have final responsibility for everything that happens in a school, but assistant principals share in differing degrees in that responsibility. Please indicate the job profile of the assistant principal(s) in your school in the following chart. Please check the "not applicable" box for any function that does not apply.

Directions:

RESPONSIBILITY	IMPORTANCE	DISCRETIONARY BEHAVIOR
In the appropriate column, indicate the **degree of responsibility** assistant principals have for each duty delegated. Circle the number: (01) Slight —The principal does the job. APs may aid at his direction. (02) Shared—Delegated with close supervision; principal and assistant principals work together. (03) Full —Delegated with general supervision; assistant principals are held responsible for the job.	In the appropriate column, indicate the **degree of importance** you believe the **delegated** duty has to the proper functioning of the school. Circle the number: (01) Least importance (02) Minor importance (03) Average importance (04) Major importance (05) Most importance	In the appropriate column, indicate your judgment of the **level of discretionary** behavior involved in the completion of any **delegated** duty in **your** school. (A duty may be of relatively minor importance and yet it could involve high discretionary behavior. The reverse may be equally true.) Circle the number: (01) Low —Behavior that is directed in large measure by others; behavior that involves restricted high order decision making. (02) High —Behavior that is self-directing, involving high order decision making.

	SAMPLE RESPONSES		
	NOT APPLICABLE	Degree of Responsibility	Degree of Importance	Level of Discretionary Behavior

Illustrated Examples Responsibility for:	N O T A P P L I C A B L E	SLIGHT	SHARED	FULL	LEAST	MINOR	AVERAGE	MAJOR	MOST	LOW	HIGH
01 Faculty Socials	☐	1	2	③	1	②	3	4.	5	1	②
02 "Career day" conferences	☐	①	2	3	1	2	3	④	5	①	2
03 Report card procedures	☑	1	2	3	1	2	3	4	5	1	2

134

Circle Appropriate Code Numbers (For an item that is not applicable to your school situation, place a check (✔) in the NA box after the item).	NOT APPLICABLE	Degree of Responsibility			Degree of Importance					Level of Discretionary Behavior	
		SLIGHT	SHARED	FULL	LEAST	MINOR	AVERAGE	MAJOR	MOST	LOW	HIGH
Responsibility for:											
Curriculum and Instruction											
(01) Articulation with feeder schools	☐	1	2	3	1	2	3	4	5	1	2
(02) Curriculum development	☐	1	2	3	1	2	3	4	5	1	2
(03) Evaluation of teachers	☐	1	2	3	1	2	3	4	5	1	2
(04) Innovations, experiments, and research	☐	1	2	3	1	2	3	4	5	1	2
(05) Instructional media and materials	☐	1	2	3	1	2	3	4	5	1	2
(06) Instructional methods	☐	1	2	3	1	2	3	4	5	1	2
(07) Instructional software	☐	1	2	3	1	2	3	4	5	1	2
(08) School-wide examinations	☐	1	2	3	1	2	3	4	5	1	2
(09) School master schedule	☐	1	2	3	1	2	3	4	5	1	2
(10) Staff inservice	☐	1	2	3	1	2	3	4	5	1	2
(11) Textbook selection	☐	1	2	3	1	2	3	4	5	1	2
(12) Work-study program	☐	1	2	3	1	2	3	4	5	1	2
Responsibility for:											
Community Relations											
(13) Administrative representative at community functions	☐	1	2	3	1	2	3	4	5	1	2
(14) Adult education program	☐	1	2	3	1	2	3	4	5	1	2
(15) Coordinating community resources for instruction	☐	1	2	3	1	2	3	4	5	1	2
(16) Informing public of school achievements	☐	1	2	3	1	2	3	4	5	1	2
(17) Liaison with community youth-serving agencies	☐	1	2	3	1	2	3	4	5	1	2
(18) Parent-Teacher Association	☐	1	2	3	1	2	3	4	5	1	2
(19) School alumni association	☐	1	2	3	1	2	3	4	5	1	2
(20) School public relations program	☐	1	2	3	1	2	3	4	5	1	2
(21) School participation in community fund drives	☐	1	2	3	1	2	3	4	5	1	2
Responsibility for:											
School Management											
(22) Building use—nonschool-related	☐	1	2	3	1	2	3	4	5	1	2
(23) Building use—school-related	☐	1	2	3	1	2	3	4	5	1	2
(24) Cafeteria services	☐	1	2	3	1	2	3	4	5	1	2
(25) Clerical services	☐	1	2	3	1	2	3	4	5	1	2
(26) Computer services	☐	1	2	3	1	2	3	4	5	1	2
(27) Custodial services	☐	1	2	3	1	2	3	4	5	1	2

	NOT APPLICABLE	Degree of Responsibility			Degree of Importance					Level of Discretionary Behavior	
Circle Appropriate Code Numbers (For an item that is not applicable to your school situation, place a check (✔) in the NA box after the item).		SLIGHT	SHARED	FULL	LEAST	MINOR	AVERAGE	MAJOR	MOST	LOW	HIGH
(28) Emergency arrangements	☐	1	2	3	1	2	3	4	5	1	2
(29) Graduation activities	☐	1	2	3	1	2	3	4	5	1	2
(30) Noninstructional equipment and supplies	☐	1	2	3	1	2	3	4	5	1	2
(31) School budget	☐	1	2	3	1	2	3	4	5	1	2
(32) School calendars	☐	1	2	3	1	2	3	4	5	1	2
(33) School daily bulletins	☐	1	2	3	1	2	3	4	5	1	2
(34) School financial accounts	☐	1	2	3	1	2	3	4	5	1	2
(35) School policies	☐	1	2	3	1	2	3	4	5	1	2
(36) Special arrangements at start and close of school year	☐	1	2	3	1	2	3	4	5	1	2
(37) Transportation services	☐	1	2	3	1	2	3	4	5	1	2

Responsibility for:

Staff Personnel

	NOT APPLICABLE	SLIGHT	SHARED	FULL	LEAST	MINOR	AVERAGE	MAJOR	MOST	LOW	HIGH
(38) Faculty meetings	☐	1	2	3	1	2	3	4	5	1	2
(39) Orientation program for new teachers	☐	1	2	3	1	2	3	4	5	1	2
(40) Student teachers	☐	1	2	3	1	2	3	4	5	1	2
(41) Substitute teachers	☐	1	2	3	1	2	3	4	5	1	2
(42) Teacher "duty" rosters	☐	1	2	3	1	2	3	4	5	1	2
(43) Teacher personnel records	☐	1	2	3	1	2	3	4	5	1	2
(44) Teacher incentives, motivation	☐	1	2	3	1	2	3	4	5	1	2
(45) Teacher selection	☐	1	2	3	1	2	3	4	5	1	2

Responsibility for:

Student Activities

	NOT APPLICABLE	SLIGHT	SHARED	FULL	LEAST	MINOR	AVERAGE	MAJOR	MOST	LOW	HIGH
(46) Assemblies	☐	1	2	3	1	2	3	4	5	1	2
(47) Athletic program	☐	1	2	3	1	2	3	4	5	1	2
(48) School club program	☐	1	2	3	1	2	3	4	5	1	2
(49) School dances	☐	1	2	3	1	2	3	4	5	1	2
(50) School newspaper	☐	1	2	3	1	2	3	4	5	1	2
(51) School traffic or safety squad	☐	1	2	3	1	2	3	4	5	1	2
(52) Student council	☐	1	2	3	1	2	3	4	5	1	2
(53) Student photographs	☐	1	2	3	1	2	3	4	5	1	2
(54) Student store	☐	1	2	3	1	2	3	4	5	1	2

Responsibility for:

Student Services

	NOT APPLICABLE	SLIGHT	SHARED	FULL	LEAST	MINOR	AVERAGE	MAJOR	MOST	LOW	HIGH
(55) Financial aid for students	☐	1	2	3	1	2	3	4	5	1	2
(56) Guidance program	☐	1	2	3	1	2	3	4	5	1	2
(57) Instruction for home-bound students	☐	1	2	3	1	2	3	4	5	1	2

Circle Appropriate Code Numbers (For an item that is not applicable to your school situation, place a check (✔) in the NA box after the item).	NOT APPLICABLE	Degree of Responsibility			Degree of Importance					Level of Discretionary Behavior	
		SLIGHT	SHARED	FULL	LEAST	MINOR	AVERAGE	MAJOR	MOST	LOW	HIGH
(58) Medical, dental, and health services	☐	1	2	3	1	2	3	4	5	1	2
(59) Orientation program for new students	☐	1	2	3	1	2	3	4	5	1	2
(60) Relationships with educational and employer representatives	☐	1	2	3	1	2	3	4	5	1	2
(61) School assistance to students in transition from school to post-school life	☐	1	2	3	1	2	3	4	5	1	2
(62) Special education (IEPs)	☐	1	2	3	1	2	3	4	5	1	2
(63) Student attendance	☐	1	2	3	1	2	3	4	5	1	2
(64) Student discipline	☐	1	2	3	1	2	3	4	5	1	2
(65) Student testing program	☐	1	2	3	1	2	3	4	5	1	2

23. Rate the influence that the following groups or individuals had on your decision to enter educational administration.

	Great Influence	Moderate Influence	Little or No Influence	Unsure or Don't Know
(01) Parents				
(02) Spouse				
(03) Colleagues				
(04) Undergraduate instructors				
(05) Graduate instructors				
(06) An administrator in your district				
(07) An administrator in another district				
(08) Friends outside of education				
(09) Others—please specify:				
(10) _____				

137

24. Rate the following as they contributed to your preparation as an assistant or vice principal.

	Great	Moderate	Little or None	Never Held
(01) Work as a teacher				
(02) Work as an adviser of a student activity				
(03) Work as a guidance counselor				
(04) Work as a department head				
(05) Participation in community activities				
(06) Participation in professional activities				
(07) Other: _____				

25. What is your perception of the importance of the following items as they contributed to your first appointment to the assistant or vice principalship?

	Very Important	Important	Of Some Importance	Of Little or No Importance
(01) Amount and quality of professional preparation				
(02) Assessment Center report				
(03) Contacts outside the profession				
(04) Contacts within the profession				
(05) I was at the right spot at the right time				
(06) Number of years of teaching experience				
(07) Performance in formal assignments outside the classroom (e.g., department head, guidance counselor)				
(08) Performance in informal assignments outside the classroom (e.g., assembly program chairman, dance moderator)				
(09) Performance on competitive exams				
(10) Success as a teacher				
(11) Success as a counselor, librarian, etc.				
(12) Successful job interview				
(13) The principal wanted me				
(14) Others—please specify: _____				
(15) _____				

138

26. To what extent did the following individuals affect the final decision by which you were appointed assistant or vice principal?

	Great Influence	Moderate Influence	Little or No Influence
(01) Principal of the school			
(02) Superintendent of the district			
(03) Board of Education			
(04) Other professional contacts			
(05) Friends			
(06) Others,—please specify:			
(07)			

27. To what degree have the circumstances listed below affected your decisions to change or not change school districts?

	An Important Factor	Of Moderate Importance	Of Little or No Importance
(01) Family commitment (i.e., number of children, nearness of relatives) motivated me to pass up or not to seek opportunities in other communities or districts			
(02) Desire to live in a certain part of the country made me more place-oriented than career-oriented			
(03) The school environment (e.g., student discipline, parental views on education) has always been an important factor in my selection of jobs.			
(04) Job security, seniority, and retirement benefits outweigh the advantages that might ensue from changing school districts.			
(05) Other factors that have influenced your career mobility. Please specify:			

28. Which of the following best describe collective bargaining's impact upon your relationships with others? *Circle all that are appropriate.*

    (01) No collective bargaining.
    (02) Enhanced my relationships with central office personnel.
    (03) Caused my relationships with central office personnel to deteriorate.
    (04) No appreciable effect on my relationship with central office personnel.
    (05) Enhanced my relationships with teachers.
    (06) Caused my relationships with teachers to deteriorate.
    (07) No appreciable effect on my relationships with teachers.

29. Please rate your degree of satisfaction with your job environment as assistant principal.

Satisfaction with:

	Very Satisfied	Satisfied	Dissatisfied	Unsure
(01) The realization of expectations you had when you took the job?				
(02) The amount of time that you devote to the job?				
(03) The results that you achieve?				
(04) The salary you receive?				
(05) The working conditions?				
(06) The amount of assistance you receive from your immediate superior(s)?				
(07) The rapport that you have with teachers?				
(08) The rapport you have with students?				
(09) The rapport you have with parents/community?				

30. Which of the following statements best reflects your present feelings about your career?

    (01) I have made good progress toward my goals.
    (02) I have made some progress toward my goals.
    (03) I have made little progress toward my goals.

31. What is your career plan for the next 3-5 years? *Select one.*

    (01) Remain in my present position.
    (02) Retirement.
    (03) Seek a central office position.
    (04) Seek a different position as a high school assistant principal.
    (05) Seek a position as a high school principal.
    (06) Seek a position as an elementary school principal.
    (07) Seek a position as a middle level principal.
    (08) Seek a position in a junior or community college.
    (09) Seek a position in a four-year institution of higher education.
    (10) Seek a position in a state department of education or other type of educational service agency (other than a school district).
    (11) Return to full time teaching.
    (12) Seek a position in a career field other than education. Please specify: _____
    (13) Other—please specify: _____
    (14) I am undecided.

32. What should be required for certification of vice principals? *Circle any item that you think should be a requirement.*
    (01) A teaching certificate
    (02) A Master's degree
    (03) A specified number of years of teaching experience
    (04) A graduate degree beyond the Master's degree
    (05) Specific courses in school administration
    (06) Specific courses in professional education other than school administration
    (07) Specific courses in curriculum development and instructional leadership
    (08) An internship or other professional field experiences
    (09) A professional examination to test knowledge of administration
    (10) Assessment of behaviors and skills (e.g., through practices such as NASSP's Assessment Center)
    (11) Monitoring after placement by professional observers to maintain certification
    (12) No requirements

33. Listed below are several factors which could be considered "roadblocks" preventing school leaders from doing the job they would like to do. Indicate by checking the appropriate boxes whether each factor has or has not been a roadblock to you during the past two years.

	Not a Factor	Somewhat a Factor	Serious Factor
(01) Collective bargaining agreement			
(02) Defective communication among administrative levels			
(03) Inability to obtain funding			
(04) Inability to provide teacher time for planning or professional development			
(05) Insufficient space and physical facilities			
(06) Lack of competent administrative assistance			
(07) Lack of competent office help			
(08) Lack of district-wide flexibility (all schools conform to same policy)			
(09) Lack of content knowledge among staff			
(10) Lack of opportunity to select staff			
(11) Lack of time for myself			
(12) Long-standing tradition in the school/district			
(13) New state guidelines/requirements			
(14) Parents apathetic or irresponsible about their children			
(15) Pressure from community			
(16) Problem students (apathetic, hostile, etc.)			
(17) Resistance to change by staff			
(18) Superintendent or central office staff who have not measured up to expectations			
(19) Teacher shortage			
(20) Teacher tenure			
(21) Teacher turnover			
(22) Time required to administer, supervise extracurricular activities			
(23) Time taken by administrative detail at expense of more important matters			
(24) Too large a student body			
(25) Too small a student body			
(26) Variations in the ability and dedication of staff			

34. Please indicate your reactions to the following broad educational issues that affect high schools across the country. Check the response after each statement which most closely reflects your view.

	Agree Without Reservation	Agree With Some Reservations	Agree With Many Reservations	Do Not Agree
(01) The principle of *universal* secondary education is essential to American society.				
(02) Federal aid must be made available to private and religious secondary schools.				
(03) Certain limitations should be placed upon classroom discussion of political "isms" and "anti-isms."				
(04) Schools require too little academic work of students. *Note:* Base your response to this item only on your own school.				
(05) Each subject taught in schools should be justifiable as practical.				
(06) Grouping according to IQ or achievement scores is desirable in academic subjects such as math, English, and foreign languages.				
(07) The academic year (compulsory) should be lengthened.				
(08) Youths who are uninterested or hostile toward schooling should not be required to attend.				
(09) School attendance should be compulsory until high school graduation or age 18.				
(10) Schools should provide a general intellectual background and leave specific job training to other agencies.				
(11) Schools should implement proven diagnostic-prescriptive strategies to personalize learning for all students.				
(12) Schools should develop special programs for educating academically talented students.				
(13) Schools should design special programs for the handicapped, ethnic minorities, and non-English-speaking.				
(14) School programs should include specific instruction on alcohol and drug abuse.				
(15) Specific criteria, based on teaching effectiveness research, should be regularly employed in teacher evaluation.				
(16) Various teacher incentives such as differential pay and career ladders should be implemented in place of salary schedules and fixed assignments.				
(17) More stringent requirements are needed for all students in the traditional academic subjects.				
(18) Standardized testing of students in all subjects is necessary to improve instruction.				
(19) Functional computer competence is essential for all students.				

Appendix B: Additional Tables

TABLE 0.1A
Distribution of Principals by Geographic Region

Geographic Region	1987	1977
New England	8	9
Mid-Atlantic	16	18
South	15	14
Midwest	39	40
Southwest	9	9
Mountain	4	3
West Coast	8	6
Non-Contiguous	1	NA

Notes: (1) The strongly similar sample distribution, while obviously not completely representative, is sufficiently similar to the 1977 survey to corroborate longitudinal comparisons.
(2) Unless otherwise stated, figures are percentages.
(3) Total across or down specific columns may not equal 100% because of normal rounding procedures.

TABLE 0.2A
Community Population

Community Type	1987	1977
City, more than 1,000,000	9	6
City, 150,000–999,999	11	8
Suburb, related to city of 150,000 or more	18	21
City, 25,000–149,999, distinct from a metropolitan area	14	16
City, 5,000–24,999, not suburban	11	20
Town or rural, under 4,999	37	28

TABLE 0.3A
School Type

Type	1987	1977	1965
Public Comprehensive	83	83	82
Public "Alternative"	1	1	NA
Public Special (Commercial, Vocational Arts, etc.)	2	2	NA
Parochial or Diocesan	4	6	7
Private, Religious-affiliated	6	7	7
Private, Not Religious-affiliated	3	1	3

Note: Very small (approximately 1%) "Other" category eliminated from 1987 responses.

TABLE 0.4A
School Size

Year	Less than 250	250 to 499	500 to 749	750 to 999	1,000 to 1,499	1,500 to 1,999	2,000 to 2,499	More than 2,500
1987	23	15	13	10	19	10	7	3
1977	—24—		16	13	20	14	—13—	
1965	—65—		11	7	8	4	— 5—	

Note: Data for 1977 and 1965 are combined at the upper and lower ends (fewer than 450 students and more than 2,000).

TABLE 0.5A
School Size by Geographic Region

Enrollment	New England	Mid-Atlantic	South	Midwest	South-west	Mountain	West Coast
Fewer than 250	6	2	19	46	12	6	6
250-499	6	12	14	44	10	6	7
500–749	11	21	18	40	5	2	3
750-999	14	23	14	43	3	1	3
1,000-1,499	10	22	15	34	7	3	8
1,500–1,999	6	20	8	35	7	0	20
2,000–2,499	2	19	13	25	27	0	15
More than 2,500	4	43	9	17	4	4	17
Region (% of nation)	8	16	15	39	9	4	8

Notes: (1) Regional categories "Non-Contiguous" and "Other" dropped for statistically insignificant response

(2) Because of the disproportionate Midwestern response, this table is best read in terms of the deviation from the regional total listed on the last line. For example, the Mid-Atlantic region has a larger share of the large schools with more than 2,500 students (43%) than its share (16%) of the total sample.

TABLE 0.6A
School Type by Size

Type	Fewer than 250	250 to 499	500 to 749	750 to 999	1,000 to 1,499	1,500 to 1,999	2,000 to 2,499	More than 2,500
Public Comprehensive								
(% of type)	4	10	14	14	27	16	10	5
(% of size)	43	73	77	80	84	93	98	92
Public Alternative								
(% of type)	14	14	29	0	29	14	0	0
(% of size)	3	2	3	0	2	1	0	0
Public Specialized								
(% of type)	0	0	14	21	43	7	0	14
(% of size)	0	0	3	4	5	1	0	8
Parochial								
(% of type)	4	24	24	16	28	0	4	0
(% of size)	3	11	8	6	5	0	2	0
Private (Religious)								
(% of type)	29	16	13	20	16	6	0	0
(% of size)	24	9	5	8	4	3	0	0
Private (Non-Religious)								
(% of type)	62	23	15	0	0	0	0	0
(% of size)	22	5	3	0	0	0	0	0
Other								
(% of type)	33	0	17	17	17	17	0	0
(% of size)	5	0	1	1	1	1	0	0

TABLE 0.7A
Grade Level Distribution

Grades	1987	1977	1965
K–12	9	2	8
1–12	1	0	17
7–12	15	6	19
8–12	2	1	6
9–12	61	63	35
10–12	9	26	12
11–12	1	1	0
Other	3	1	1

TABLE 1.1A
Distribution of Principals by Sex

Sex	1987	1977	1965
Female	12	7	10
Male	88	93	89

TABLE 1.3A
Sex of Principals by Region

Principals	Nation	New England	Mid-Atlantic	South	Midwest	South-west	Mountain	West Coast
Male	88	93	86	89	89	91	92	80
Female	12	7	14	11	11	9	8	20

TABLE 1.4A
Sex of Assistant Principals by Region

Assistant Principals	Nation	New England	Mid-Atlantic	South	Midwest	South-west	Mountain	West Coast
Male	82	78	84	73	85	88	93	74
Female	18	22	16	27	15	12	7	26

Notes: (1) Statistically small "Non-Contiguous" and "Other" categories dropped.
(2) All numbers refer to percentages unless otherwise stated.
(3) Percentages in specific rows or columns may not total 100 due to rounding procedures.
(4) Because of the complexity of data and the occasional incompatibility in the items, the following rule for presentation of data was followed in most cases:
   (a) When considering a single variable, data are depicted longitudinally where earlier data are available. In these cases, data on assistant principals, if available, are presented in a parallel table.
   (b) When considering cross tabulations of variables, data for both principals and assistant principals, if available, are presented in an integrated format.

TABLE 1.5A
Sex of Principals and Assistant Principals by Community Population

Sex	Nation		City 1,000,000+		City 999,999–150,000		Suburb 15,000+		City 149,999-25,000		City 24,999-5,000		Town/ Rural 4,999 or fewer	
	P	AP	P	AP	P	AP	P	AP	P	AP	P	AP	P	AP
Female	12	18	34	33	26	28	9	22	9	15	10	9	4	11
Male	88	82	66	67	74	72	91	78	91	85	90	91	96	89

TABLE 1.6A
Sex of Principals and Assistant Principals by School Type

Sex	National		Public Compreh.		Public Altern.		Public Special.		Parochial		Private Religious		Private Non-Relig.	
	P	AP	P	AP	P	AP	P	AP	P	AP	P	AP	P	AP
Female	12	18	8	16	60	0	27	36	30	24	30	36	21	38
Male	88	82	92	84	40	100	73	64	70	76	70	64	79	62

148

TABLE 1.7A
Distribution of Principals by Age

	24-29	30–34	35–39	40–44	45–49	50–54	55–59	60+
1987	0	3	16	24	21	19	11	5
1977	1	8	16	22	22	19	8	5
1965	4	12	18	16	15	15	12	8

TABLE 1.9A
Age of Principals and Assistant Principals by Region

Age	Nation		New England		Mid-Atlantic		South		Midwest		South-west		Mountain		West Coast	
	P	AP	P	AP	P	AP	P	AP	P	AP	P	AP	P	AP	P	AP
20–39	19	29	26	13	9	29	25	30	21	32	15	29	29	27	17	25
40–49	45	45	35	60	49	46	50	41	46	45	47	44	29	40	44	35
50+	35	27	39	27	42	26	25	29	33	23	38	26	42	33	39	39

Note: Categories "Non-Contiguous" and "Other" dropped.

TABLE 1.10A
Age of Principals and Assistant Principals by Community Population

Age	City 1,000,000+		City 999,999–150,000		Suburb 15,000+		City 149,999–25,000		City 24,999–5,000		Town/Rural 4,999 or fewer	
	P	AP	P	AP	P	AP	P	AP	P	AP	P	AP
20–39	10	18	9	17	17	25	12	20	27	40	26	46
40–49	26	51	38	49	50	50	45	54	49	40	49	29
50+	64	31	53	34	33	25	43	26	24	20	24	25

TABLE 1.11A
Ethnic Distribution of Principals

	White	Black	Hispanic	American Indian	Asian	Other
1987	93.7	3.8	1.7	.1	.4	.3
1977	96	3	.6	.2	.2	0

TABLE 1.13A
Ethnicity of Principals by Region

	Nation		New England		Mid-Atlantic		South		Midwest		South-west		Mountain		West Coast	
	P	AP	P	AP	P	AP	P	AP	P	AP	P	AP	P	AP	P	AP
Non-white	6	11	0	3	4	11	7	24	5	7	11	18	0	0	20	10
White	94	89	100	97	96	89	93	76	95	93	89	82	100	100	80	90

TABLE 1.14A
Ethnicity of Principals and Assistant Principals by Community Population

	Nation		City 1,000,000+		City 999,999–150,000		Suburb 15,000+		City 149,999–25,000		City 24,999–5,000		Town/Rural 4,999 or fewer	
	P	AP	P	AP	P	AP	P	AP	P	AP	P	AP	P	AP
Non-White	6	11	15	22	19	23	5	5	9	12	4	3	2	8
White	94	89	85	78	81	77	95	95	91	88	96	97	98	92

TABLE 1.17A
Basis for Determining Salary

Basis	Principal	Assistant Principal
By Board, on Superintendent's Recommendation, Without Consultation or Negotiation	30	29
By a Formal Bargaining Group	16	23
By Informal Negotiation with the Board as an Administrative Group	13	8
By Informal and Individual Negotiation with the Board	11	2
Other	9	14
By Informal Negotiation with the Superintendent as an Administrative Group	8	9
By Informal and Individual Negotiation with the Superintendent	5	3
By Board Without Consultation or Negotiation	5	9
By Superintendent, Without Consultation or Negotiation	4	3

TABLE 1.18A
Salaries of Principals and Assistant Principals by Age

Age	Less than $30,000		$30,000–$44,999		$45,000 or More	
	P	AP	P	AP	P	AP
34 or younger	56	53	42	45	2	2
35–39	9	21	62	69	25	10
40–44	8	13	53	74	37	13
45–49	7	10	42	70	50	21
50–54	8	11	31	50	59	39
55 or older	5	19	30	59	62	22

Note: "Does Not Apply: Religious" salary category eliminated.

TABLE 1.19A
Salaries of Principals and Assistant Principals by Ethnicity

	Less than $30,000		$30,000–$44,999		$45,000 or More	
Ethnicity	P	AP	P	AP	P	AP
White	9	17	46	64	43	19
Non-White	2	13	20	73	77	15

Note: "Does Not Apply: Religious" salary category eliminated.

TABLE 1.20A
Salaries of Principals by Region

Region	Less than $25,000	$25,000–29,999	$30,000–34,999	$35,000–39,999	$40,000–44,999	$45,000–49,999	$50,000–54,999	$55,000–59,999	$60,000 or more
New England	5	2	16	14	23	32	4	0	5
Mid-Atlantic	2	2	2	8	11	20	21	8	20
South	7	9	15	19	19	13	8	3	5
Midwest	5	6	14	15	21	12	15	6	4
Southwest	2	6	14	17	20	14	17	8	3
Mountain	0	8	20	16	28	16	8	4	0
West Coast	2	0	5	9	10	22	26	14	12

Notes: (1) Regional categories "Non-Contiguous" and "Other" eliminated from table.
(2) Salary category "Does Not Apply: Religious Order" eliminated from table.

TABLE 1.21A
Salaries of Assistant Principals by Region

Region	Less than $20,000	$20,000–24,999	$25,000–29,999	$30,000–34,999	$35,000–39,999	$40,000–44,999	$45,000–49,999	$50,000–54,999	$55,000 or more
New England	5	8	3	10	33	26	5	0	5
Mid-Atlantic	2	1	3	20	22	20	12	7	9
South	4	12	17	24	26	13	2	0	0
Midwest	2	4	12	21	21	22	10	5	1
Southwest	3	3	9	19	28	18	9	12	0
Mountain	7	0	7	13	47	20	0	7	0
West Coast	0	2	2	10	14	33	22	16	0

Notes: (1) Regional categories "Non-Contiguous" and "Other" eliminated from table.
(2) Salary category "Does Not Apply: Religious Order" eliminated from table.

TABLE 1.22A
Salaries of Principals and Assistant Principals by Sex

	Nation		Less than $25,000		$25,000–29,999		$30,000–34,999		$35,000–39,999		$40,000–44,999		$45,000–49,999		$50,000–54,999		$55,000–59,999		$60,000 or more	
Sex	P	AP	P	AP	P	AP	P	AP	P	AP	P	AP	P	AP	P	AP	P	AP	P	AP
Male	88	81	75	63	83	87	98	86	94	84	88	79	94	80	79	87	86	69	89	NA
Female	12	19	25	37	17	13	2	14	6	16	12	21	6	20	21	13	14	31	11	NA

Notes: (1) Assistant Principal salary scales are slightly lower than the Principal scales ($5,000 across each range). Thus, the top end of A.P. scales was "$55,000 or more," which is shown here under "$55,000–$59,999." Some assistant principals could have been above $60,000.
(2) As before, religious category excluded from salary range.

TABLE 1.23A
Salaries of Principals and Assistant Principals by School Size

	Less than $30,000		$30,000–$39,999		$40,000–$49,999		$50,000 or more	
Enrollment	P	AP	P	AP	P	AP	P	AP
499 or fewer	73	59	39	15	6	3	2	2
500–999	23	31	40	41	28	17	8	7
1,000–1,999	4	8	19	37	51	57	62	63
2,000 or more	0	2	3	7.	14	23	29	28

TABLE 1.24A
Fringe Benefits of Principals and Assistant Principals

	Medical	Retire.	Life Insurance	Dental	Auto or Mileage	Tuition for self	Expense Account	Meals	Tuition for Dependents	Housing	None
Principals	87	68	64	58	55	17	11	10	5	4	5
Assistant Principals	83	65	65	60	42	18	2	8	4	2	6

TABLE 1.25A
Length of Contract for Principals and Assistant Principals

	9–9.5 months	10–10.5 months	11–11.5 months	12 months
Principals	1	17	23	59
Assistant Principals	6	34	23	38

TABLE 1.26A
Multi-Year Contracts for Principals and Assistant Principals

	Annual Only	Two Years	Three Years	More than Three Years
Principals	58	25	11	5
Assistant Principals	64	18	14	4

TABLE 1.27A
Membership in Civic Organizations
for Principals and Assistant Principals

	None	One	Two	Three	Four	Five or more
Principals	34	23	26	12	4	1
Assistant Principals	38	26	21	10	3	2

TABLE 1.28A
Membership in Professional Organizations
for Principals and Assistant Principals

	NASSP and its affiliates	NASSP plus 1 other	NASSP plus 2 others	NASSP plus 3 others	Others but not NASSP
Principals	18	23	27	16	15
Assistant Principals	21	20	13	11	36

TABLE 1.29A
District Support for Principals' and Assistant Principals' Professional
Development Activities

	Grants Released Time	Pays Most or All Expenses	Pays Member Dues	Encourages at Principal's Own Expense	Pays Less Than 50% of Expenses	Discourages Participation
Principals	78	55	43	42	22	4
Assistant Principals	73	52	27	52	16	5

TABLE 2.2A
School Size by Administration Team Size

	Number of Assistant Principals			
Enrollment	0	1	2	3 or more
Fewer than 499	67	40	3	4
500–749	17	27	15	0
750–999	17	17	23	5
1,000–1,499	0	14	43	25
1,500–1,999	0	0	9	30
2,000 or more	0	2	8	36

153

TABLE 2.3A
School Size by Adequacy of Administrative Support

Enrollment	Inadequate	Adequate	More Than Adequate
Fewer than 499	35	47	19
500–749	14	50	36
750–999	29	21	50
1,000–1,499	25	33	42
1,500–1,999	25	25	50
2,000 or more	39	41	20

TABLE 2.4A
Average Work Week of Principals

Hours per Week	1987	1977	1965
60 or more	27	22	29
55 to 59	27		
50 to 54	32	61	45
45 to 49	12		
40 to 44	2	17	17
Fewer than 40	0	0	8

TABLE 2.7A
Teaching Responsibility of Principals and Assistant Principals

	1987 Prin.	1987 Asst. Prin.	1977 Prin.	1965 Prin.
None	88	85	85	65
One or more courses	12	15	15	35

Notes: (1) "Yes" responses collapsed from "one course" and "two to three courses" in 1987.
(2) "Yes" responses collapsed from "Incidentally, by choice," "less than half time but regularly," and "more than half-time" in 1977.
(3) "Yes" responses for 1965 collapsed from "less than half-time" and "more than half-time."

TABLE 2.8A
Informal Classroom Visits

		(Hours per Week)		
None	1–3 hours	4–6 hours	7–9 hours	10 or more hours
0	33	45	12	10

TABLE 2.9A
Scope of Principals' Authority

Function	Unrestricted Authority		Moderately Restricted Authority		Little Authority		No Authority	
	1987	1977	1987	1977	1987	1977	1987	1977
Allocation of discretionary funds	20	19	67	58	11	16	3	6
Budget allocation	39	37	23	30	23	21	16	12
Staffing practices	12	16	46	51	30	20	12	12
Staff selection	40	51	27	41	28	0	5	8

TABLE 2.11A
Administrative Roadblocks for Principals and Assistant Principals

Problem	Principal	Asst. Principal
Time taken up by administrative detail	83	81
Lack of time	79	73
Inability to obtain funds	76	76
Apathetic or irresponsible parents	70	70
New state guidelines and requirements	69	59
Time to administer/supervise student activities	68	63
Variations in the ability of teachers	64	70
Inability to provide teacher time for prof. dev.	62	58
Insufficient space and physical facilities	61	58
Resistance to change by staff	57	69
Problem students	55	67
Defective communications among admin. levels	55	64
Longstanding traditions	51	41
Collective bargaining agreement	45	44
Teacher tenure	42	38
Community pressure	34	42
Lack of district-wide flexibility	33	38
Supt./central office staff do not measure up to expectations	32	41
Lack of competent administrative assistance	29	25
Teacher shortage	29	33
Lack of competent office help	27	30
Lack of opportunity to select staff	21	39
Teacher turnover	21	29
Student body too small	20	10
Lack of content knowledge among staff	16	25
Student body too large	15	17

TABLE 2.12A
Incidence of Collective Bargaining

None	Teachers Only	Administrators Only	Teachers and Administrators Only	All Employees
38	31	1	6	24

155

TABLE 2.13A
Impact of Collective Bargaining

	Principal	Asst. Principal
No collective bargaining	38	34
Enhanced relationships with central office	5	8
Detracted from relationships with central office	5	3
No change in relationships with central office	33	39
Enhanced relationships with teachers	5	10
Detracted from relationships with teachers	12	6
No change in relationships with teachers	39	47

TABLE 2.15A
Parent/Community Involvement

Area	Percentage of Principals Who Feel Parents/Community Should Be Involved
Fund raising for a school-based foundation	64
Fund raising for individual school projects	61
Volunteer services for general administrative tasks	54
Development of rules and procedures for student discipline	53
Supervision of student activities	49
Curriculum development	36
Student activity program planning	32
Evaluation of school or classroom climate	29
Instructional assistance in the classrooms	26
Review committees for appeals on student rights and responsibilities	24
Review and evaluation of school grading and reporting practices	22
Review and evaluation of instructional materials	21
Evaluation of curriculum or instruction	21
Selection of school personnel	6
Evaluation of school personnel	3

TABLE 2.16A
Influence of Interest Groups on Principals

Group	1987	1977	1965
Athletic boosters (especially alumni)	61	48	51
Band/Music boosters	61	NA	NA
Teachers' organizations	60	40	NA
State colleges and/or universities	50	13	46
PTA or PTO	49	NA	NA
Citizen or parent groups (non-PTA)	43	34	56
Business community	40	39	45
Local middle level schools	40	NA	NA
Local elementary schools	37	NA	NA
Local media	32	24	31
Religious or church groups	31	17	35
Individuals, groups concerned about national reports, school reform	21	11	30
Individuals, groups concerned about testing program	16	12	33
Women's or minority rights organizations	12	13	NA
Local labor organizations	10	3	3
Extremist individuals or groups (right or left)	7	13	30
Legal aid groups	6	5	NA
Censorship groups (books, programs, etc.)	4	5	17

Note: Percentages combine responses expressing either "moderate" or "extreme" influence.

TABLE 2.18A
Principal and Assistant Principal Ratings of Job Characteristics

Job Characteristic		Principal	Asst. Principal
Job Security:	"Little"	11	11
	"Moderate"	26	25
	"Considerable"	64	65
Opportunity To Help Others:	"Little"	2	1
	"Moderate"	9	11
	"Considerable"	89	89
Prestige:	"Little"	5	13
	"Moderate"	27	50
	"Considerable"	69	37
Independent Thought & Action:	"Little"	7	8
	"Moderate"	27	30
	"Considerable"	66	62
Self-Fulfillment:	"Little"	6	15
	"Moderate"	28	25
	"Considerable"	66	61

Notes: (1) Percentages are for "actual" ratings of the characteristics; percentages for "ideal" ratings were always higher than the "actual" ratings, but there was no significant shift in the ideal ratings since 1977; thus their omission.

(2) A five-point scale was used: "Little" responses combine choices 1&2, "Considerable" responses combine 4&5.

TABLE 3.2A
Expenditure per Student by Region

Region	Less than $1,500	$1,500 to $1,999	$2,000 to $2,499	$2,500 to $2,999	$3,000 to $3,499	$3,500 to $3,999	$4,000 to $4,499	$4,500 to $4,999	More than $5,000	% of Total Sample
New England	0	7	8	10	9	5	16	15	9	8
Mid-Atlantic	14	6	11	16	21	20	26	23	35	16
South	43	27	16	8	7	8	10	8	9	15
Midwest	14	41	46	40	43	46	32	31	26	39
Southwest	14	10	9	13	7	7	6	8	2	9
Mountain	5	6	1	3	1	3	3	8	9	3
West Coast	10	2	6	11	11	10	6	8	5	8
Non-Contiguous	0	1	<1	0	0	0	0	0	5	<1
Other	0	0	1	0	0	2	0	0	0	0
% of Total Sample	6	13	21	22	15	9	5	2	7	100

TABLE 3.5A
Graduates Entering College

High Schools	1987 Graduates	1977 Graduates	1965 Graduates
95.0 or more	7	3	4
80.0 to 94.9	13	7	5
60.0 to 79.9	24	18	13
40.0 to 59.9	31 (75)*	34 (62)*	25 (37)*
30.0 to 49.9	12	21	21
20.0 to 29.9	8	11	15
10.0 to 19.9	3	5	9
Less than 10.0	2	1	6

*Cumulative percentage

TABLE 3.7A
Teacher Preparations

Teachers	Schools 1 Preparation	2 Preparations	3 Preparations	4 or More Preparations
76 to 100	7	9	5	7
51 to 75	9	15	9	5
26 to 50	7	31	30	8
1 to 25	49	31	40	38
None	28	15	16	42

158

TABLE 3.8A
Full-Time Subject Supervisors

Subject Area	Supervisors
Agriculture	11
Business Education	30
Computer Literacy/Skills	24
English/Language Arts	39
Fine Arts (Art, Music, Theater)	32
Foreign Languages	30
Home Economics	28
Mathematics	36
Physical Education	32
Science	35
Social Sciences	36
Vocational Education	35

TABLE 3.9A
Percentage of Full-Time Male Teachers

Male Teachers	1987	1977	1965
Less than 10%	3	3	7
10–19	4	3	3
20–29	4	4	4
30–39	15	10	8
40–49	23 (49)*	16 (36)*	14 (36)*
50–59	26	29	21
60–69	16	24	21
70–79	4	7	11
80–89	4	4	11
90–100	<1		

*Cumulative percentage

TABLE 3.10A
Influence on Selection of Content and Materials

| Influence Group | Area of Influence | | |
	Subject Content	Textbooks	Library Books
Teachers	72	80	77
Principal/School Administrators	12	7	7
District Supervisors	11	9	11
School Board	3	3	1
Parents	1	1	1
No opinion/Not sure	2	0	4

TABLE 3.11A
Graduation Requirement Trends by Subject Area

Subjects	Decreased	Same	Increased
Agriculture	4	94	2
Business Education	7	81	12
Computer Literacy/Skills	0	46	53
English/Language Arts	0	59	41
Fine Arts	4	65	32
Foreign Languages	1	70	29
Home Economics	12	84	5
Mathematics	0	25	75
Physical Education	18	75	7
Science	0	34	66
Social Sciences	1	63	36
Vocational Education	9	84	7

TABLE 3.12A
Graduation Elective Credit Trends

Credit Hours Toward Graduation	
Elective hours increased	35
Elective hours decreased	47
Elective hours stayed the same	18

TABLE 3.13A
Incidence of Tracking

Programs of Study	Tracking
College preparatory	45
General	35
Vocational-technical	20
Does not apply (No formal tracking)	54

TABLE 3.14A
Grouping Practices by Subject Areas

Subjects	Assignment Practice				
	Grade Point Average	Standardized Tests	Student Interest or Choice	Teacher Recommendation	No Special Criteria
(01) Agriculture	1	0	35	8	20
(02) Business Education	5	2	72	30	24
(03) Computer Literacy/Skills	8	3	60	27	24
(04) English/Language Arts	28	36	49	62	16
(05) Fine Arts	3	1	66	23	25
(06) Foreign Languages	17	8	71	41	14
(07) Home Economics	0	1	66	10	26
(08) Mathematics	33	40	55	73	11
(09) Physical Education	0	0	46	8	49
(10) Science	26	27	62	61	13
(11) Social Sciences	12	10	56	37	28
(12) Vocational Education	3	4	66	20	25

TABLE 3.16A
Criteria for Gifted/Talented Programs

Practice	
Selection is by teacher nomination or recommendation	61
Selection is based on standardized achievement tests	47
Selection is based on prior grade point average	42
Selection is by student choice and interest	40
Selection is based on standardized aptitude tests	26
Students may be dropped from program based on their grades	35
Students may be dropped from program based on standardized achievement test performance	11
Students may be dropped from program based on subsequent standardized aptitude test performance	8

TABLE 3.18A
Students Participating in Community-Based Programs

Students Participating	
0–19	79
20–39	15
40–59	4
60–79	2
80–100	0

TABLE 3.22A
Educational Initiatives

	Already well established involvement	Strong new initiatives	Moderate new initiatives	Little or no activity
Instruction				
Clarification of instructional goals and priorities	38	37	22	3
Diagnosis of student learning styles	8	21	39	32
Monitoring of student progress, e.g., competency testing, outcomes-based education	25	34	34	7
Recognition of student academic achievement	43	38	18	1
Steps to enhance instructional standards and expectations	34	48	17	1
Steps to minimize interruptions of classes and instructional activities	39	24	32	5
Updating of curriculum and instructional resources	38	41	19	2
Others	20	40	20	20
Instructional Staff				
Direct supervision and consultation	52	31	16	1
Evaluation of instruction	50	33	16	1
Inservice education	22	31	37	10
Involvement in curriculum development	37	30	28	5
Involvement in planning for instructional improvement	41	37	19	3
Involvement in school policy development	39	32	21	8
Teacher incentives, e.g., career ladders, released time, etc.	10	19	30	41
Others	17	50	17	16
Students and Student Relations				
Activities to recognize student achievements and enhance student attitudes	36	38	24	2
Improvement of counseling services and procedures	30	31	28	11
Involvement in school policy making and problem solving	37	29	24	10
Review of attendance policies and procedures	37	30	26	7
Review of discipline rules and procedures	40	33	20	7
Others	0	25	50	25

162

TABLE 3.22A (CONTINUED)
Educational Initiatives

	Already well established involvement	Strong new initiatives	Moderate new initiatives	Little or no activity
Administrative Central Office				
Improved administrative operations, e.g., use of computers, non-instructional staff	26	43	25	6
Involvement in long-range planning	20	30	34	15
Preparation of proposals and recommendations for school improvement, e.g., articulation with other schools	21	26	39	14
Recommended changes in school operations and procedures, e.g., schedule of school day, student progress reporting	29	21	33	16
Others	0	25	50	25
Parent/Community Relations				
Parent conferencing	40	19	27	13
Parent/community volunteers and aides in the school	17	13	27	43
Parental/community participation in policy making and problem solving	16	20	32	33
Strategies for improved communication, e.g., contacts with those who have no children in school	10	16	29	45
Use of community facilities and resources	25	16	32	27
Others	0	0	0	100
Innovative Programs (Please list and rate)	39	53	4	3
	33	61	0	5
	29	47	6	18

163